# VALUE & PEACE EDUCATION

## EMPOWERING MINDS FOR PEACEFUL CO-EXISTENCE


MOHD SALAHUDDIN QAZI,
FIRDOSE A. MIR, BILAL A. SHAH
SABA WAJHIE
IQRA HAFEEZ

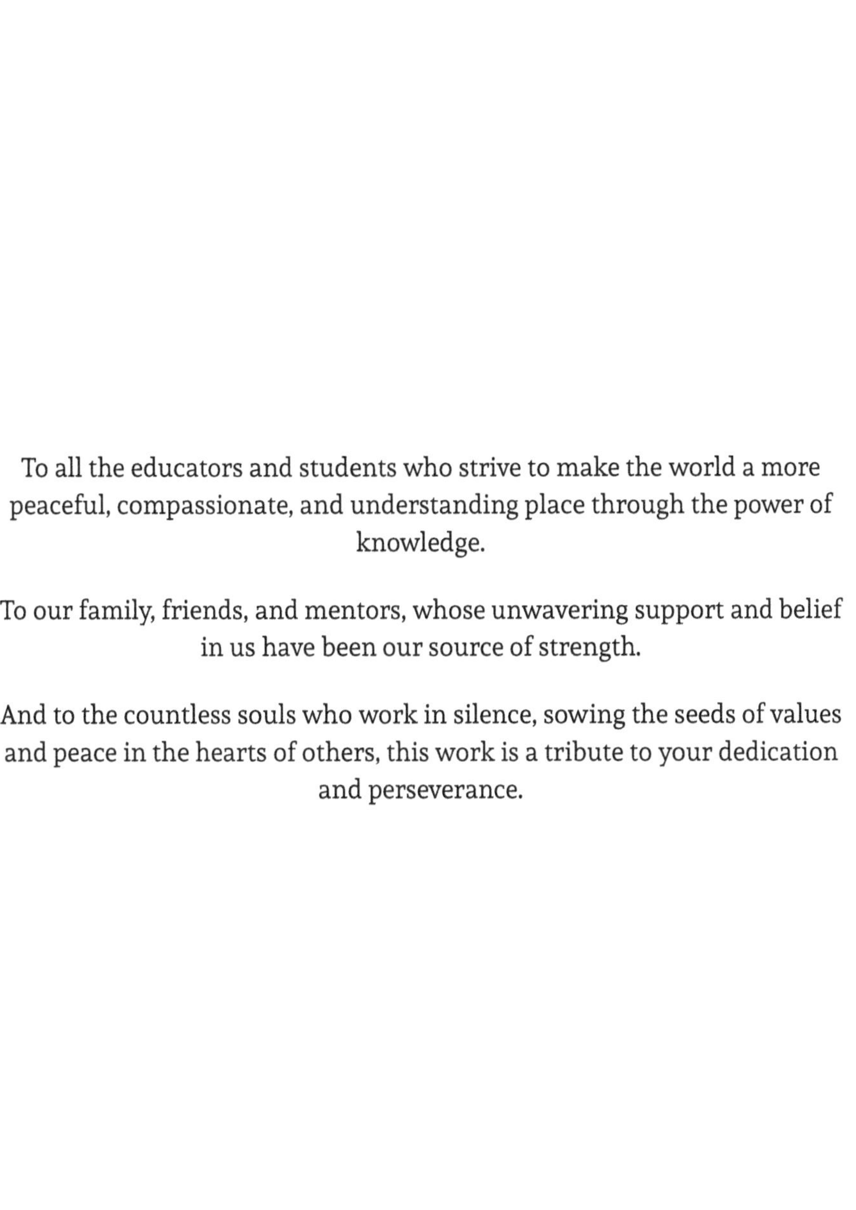

To all the educators and students who strive to make the world a more peaceful, compassionate, and understanding place through the power of knowledge.

To our family, friends, and mentors, whose unwavering support and belief in us have been our source of strength.

And to the countless souls who work in silence, sowing the seeds of values and peace in the hearts of others, this work is a tribute to your dedication and perseverance.

# Contents

# PREFACE

In a world marked by rapid change and diverse challenges, the need for a foundational education in values and peace has never been more urgent. *Value & Peace Education* is a response to this growing need, aiming to cultivate the principles of compassion, empathy, and understanding within individuals and society at large. We, the authors—**Mohd Salahuddin Qazi, Firdose A. Mir, Bilal Ahmad Shah, Saba Wajhie,** and **Iqra Hafeez**—have collaborated on this book to provide a guide for educators, students, and all those who aspire to live and promote peaceful coexistence in their communities.

This book delves into the core elements of value-based education, exploring how personal and social values can be nurtured through thoughtful and intentional teaching practices. Recognizing that peace is not merely the absence of conflict but a state of mutual respect, we discuss ways to integrate peace-building techniques into educational frameworks. By presenting a blend of theory, practical applications, and insights from various cultural perspectives, we aim to make the concepts accessible and relevant to readers from all walks of life.

Our journey in creating this book has been driven by a shared belief that education is a powerful tool for transforming societies. Through Value & Peace Education, we hope to inspire educators to instill these values in the hearts and minds of future generations, ultimately fostering a more ethical and peaceful world.

We would like to extend our gratitude to the readers and educators who embrace these ideals and strive to make a difference. It is our sincere hope that this book serves as a resource and inspiration for all who seek to bring about positive change in society through education grounded in values and peace.

— The Authors

# ACKNOWLEDGEMENTS

We — **Mohd Salahuddin Qazi, Firdose A. Mir, Bilal Ahmad Shah, Saba Wajhie and Iqra Hafeez,** are grateful to all those who have supported us in bringing "**Value & Peace Education**" to life. This book reflects the collective efforts, insights, and dedication of many individuals who have guided and inspired us throughout the journey.

First and foremost, we would like to thank our families, friends, and mentors, whose encouragement and unwavering belief in our vision provided the foundation for this work. Their patience and understanding have been invaluable as we devoted countless hours to research, writing, and refining our ideas.

We also extend our gratitude to the educators, colleagues, and students who have engaged with us in meaningful discussions on values and peace. Their feedback and perspectives have enriched our understanding and strengthened the ideas presented in this book.

Finally, we acknowledge all those who work tirelessly to promote values and peace within their communities and classrooms. It is our hope that this book serves as both a guide and an inspiration for those committed to creating a more harmonious world through education.

Thank you for joining us on this journey toward a compassionate, ethical, and peaceful society.

- *The Authors*

# CONTENT

**Title : Value & Peace Education**
**Course Contents**
**Unit I**

**Introduction to Peace Education**

1. Peace Education: Concept and Need
2. Peace contexts: underlying assumptions , processes
3. Approaches to Peace Education

**Unit II**
**Peace Education & Prominent Educationists**

1. Peace Education for National Integration and International Integration
2. Peace Education propagated by Gandhi, Aurbindo, Swami Vivekanand
3. NCF 2005 recommendations on Peace Education.

**Unit III**
**Human Rights & Fundamental Rights**

1. Historical Background of Human Rights
2. Fundamental Rights as included in Indian Constitution
3. Human Rights protection in Indian Constitution.

**Unit IV**
**Teaching Methods & Activities**

1. Methods & activities of Teaching Human Rights
2. Obstacles of Human Rights Education
3. National Human Rights Commission (NHRC), State Human Rights Commission (SHRC).

**Unit V**
**Adult Education and Distance Education**

1. Concept, Need and Importance of Adult Education and Life Long

Learning
2. National Literacy Mission (NLM) & Total Literacy Campaign (TLC)
3. Meaning, Need and Importance of Open and Distance Learning (ODL)
4. Sailent features of Distance Education
5. Open University System.

# Unit VI
## Value Education & Enviromental Education

1. Meaning , Need and Importance of Human Values
2. Classification , development and inclusion of human values
3. Nature, meaning and importance of Environmental Education
4. Programmes of Environmental Education.

# Unit VII
## Population Education

1. Meaning, importance and objectives of Population Education
2. Population explosion, its causes and impact
3. Population Growth and problems of unemployment

# Unit VIII
## Inclusive Education

1. Meaning, objectives and principles and importance
2. Socially disadvantaged children, meaning and characteristics
3. Learning disability, meaning, characteristics and classification
4. Educational provisions and role of teacher.

# I

# Introduction to Peace Education

*When we hear "peace," the first thing we think of is the opposite of war. From there, we think of any "resolution of conflict," including arguments at home. Conflicts are solved. That's "peace."*

## 1.1 Concept and Need of Peace Education

*Peace education* goes beyond the concept of making a living. It teaches the students how to maintain harmony and peace in the world and have critical and logical thinking. The main concept of peace education is to make people aware of the importance of peacemaking and to develop a positive environment. Peace education is a concept that involves the teaching and learning of skills, attitudes, and knowledge that promote peace and non-violent conflict resolution. It is a process that aims to build a culture of peace by transforming the way people think and act towards each other and the world around them. Peace education encompasses a broad range of subjects and topics, including human rights, conflict resolution, social justice, sustainable development, gender equality, and intercultural understanding. It emphasizes the importance of critical thinking, empathy, and dialogue as tools for resolving conflicts peacefully. The goals of peace education are to empower individuals and communities to become agents of positive change, to promote social cohesion and respect for diversity, and to create a more just and peaceful world. It is a lifelong process that can take place in formal and non-formal educational settings, as well as in families, communities, and through social media. Peace education seeks to create a world in which conflicts are resolved nonviolently, human rights are respected, and all individuals are able to live in peace and dignity.

Peace education is an approach to learning that focuses on building a culture of peace through the acquisition of knowledge, skills, attitudes, and values. It involves educating individuals, communities, and societies to understand and practice peaceful ways of resolving conflicts, promoting social justice, and preventing violence.

Peace education aims to foster a sense of empathy and compassion, promote critical thinking and problem-solving skills, and encourage respect for diversity and human rights. It seeks to create a world where people can coexist peacefully and conflicts can be resolved without resorting to violence.

The ultimate goal of peace education is to create a sustainable culture of peace, where people are empowered to address issues such as poverty, inequality, and injustice, and work together to build peaceful and harmonious societies.

"Peace education is the process of acquiring knowledge, skills, attitudes, and values necessary to bring about a culture of peace and nonviolence."

Peace education is a broad and multi-faceted field, and there are many definitions given by educationists on what it encompasses. Here are some of the commonly cited definitions:

"Peace education is an interdisciplinary field of inquiry and action that aims to develop the knowledge, skills, and attitudes needed to create a culture of peace." - ***Betty Reardon***

"Peace education involves teaching about the causes of conflict, the skills of conflict resolution, and the conditions necessary for a culture of peace." - ***UNESCO***

"Peace education is the process of promoting the knowledge, skills, attitudes and values needed to bring about behaviour changes that will enable individuals, groups and societies to resolve conflicts in a non-violent manner." - ***Douglas P. Fry***

"Peace education aims to foster a sense of empathy, respect for diversity, critical thinking, and a commitment to social justice and nonviolent action." - ***Ian Harris***

"Peace education is the process of empowering individuals with the values, knowledge, and skills to resolve conflicts in a peaceful manner, and to promote social justice and human rights." - ***Nel Noddings***

These above definitions highlight the importance of promoting peace through education and the need to develop the knowledge, skills, attitudes, and values necessary for creating a culture of peace. Peace education involves teaching about conflict resolution, social justice, human rights, empathy, and critical thinking.

**Some key points to help understand the concept and need for peace education:**

Peace education is an interdisciplinary approach that draws on various fields, including psychology, sociology, philosophy, and education.

It seeks to promote peace, justice, human rights, and sustainable development through education.

1) It emphasizes the importance of understanding and managing conflicts nonviolently and creatively.

2) It is aimed at developing skills and attitudes that enable individuals to resolve conflicts constructively, cooperate with others, and build positive relationships.

3) It involves developing empathy, critical thinking, problem-solving, communication, and leadership skills.

**1.1.1) Seven pillars of peace education :**

**A) Community Building:-** Finding things that unite and bind us together as a group, while at the same time respecting and celebrating our differences. Embracing the interests, experiences, and goals of the community to shape the learning environment and gain ownership of the learning experience.

**B) Enabling Multiple Intelligences:-** Balancing the learning experience by engaging learners in ways that play to their strengths while also challenging them to develop other intelligences.

**C) Nurturing Emotional Intelligence:-** Acknowledging the emotions, feelings, and experiences that each learner brings to the learning environment and helping them find ways to cope with those emotions. Also, nurturing compassion and empathy among students in ways that allow them to be sensitive and aware of each other's emotions.

**D) Exploring Approaches to Peace:-** Breaking the ideal, overarching concept of peace into manageable bites and methods of actualization.

**E) Reframing History:-** Challenging the dominance of violence and war in the narratives of cultures, countries, and peoples. Changing the lens through which we look at major historical shifts, construct heroes, and develop cultural norms.

**F) Transforming Conflict Nonviolently**:- Embracing the inevitability of conflict by practicing nonviolent ways to wage it, manage it, and resolve it.

**G) Skill Building**:- All these pillars are held together and buttressed by the end goal of building, practicing, and adopting life skills that empower individuals to bring about peace in the world around them – interpersonal skills, intrapersonal skills, analytical skills, conflict resolution skills, organizing skills, and learning skills.

**1.2 ) Need for Peace Education:**

1) In today's world, there are various forms of conflicts, violence, and wars, which cause significant human suffering, loss of lives, and destruction of property.

2) Peace education can help create a culture of peace and nonviolence, which is essential for the well-being and survival of humanity.

3) It can contribute to the prevention of conflicts and the promotion of dialogue, tolerance, and mutual understanding.

4) It can help to reduce social inequalities, discrimination, and exclusion, which are often the root causes of conflicts.

5) Peace education is needed to ensure that future generations understand the importance of peace and have the skills and attitudes necessary to maintain it.

6) It is a tool for promoting global citizenship and fostering a sense of responsibility for the well-being of the planet and all its inhabitants.

Peace education is essential for building a better and more peaceful world. It is a process of acquiring knowledge, developing attitudes, and learning skills that promote peaceful coexistence and nonviolent conflict resolution. Here are some reasons why peace education is important and necessary:

- **Reducing violence:** Peace education is a proactive approach to reducing violence. By teaching individuals how to handle conflicts peacefully, it helps to reduce the incidence of violence in schools, homes, and communities. *Reducing violence* is essential for prevailing peace because violence often creates a cycle of retaliation and retribution, leading to further violence and instability. When violence occurs, it can cause physical harm, psychological trauma, and damage to property and infrastructure. This can lead to a breakdown of trust between individuals, groups, and communities, and make it more difficult to build and maintain peaceful relationships. Reducing violence can also create an environment that is more conducive to dialogue and negotiation. When violence is present, people may feel threatened and unsafe, making it difficult for them to engage in meaningful communication or conflict resolution. By reducing violence, it can become easier for individuals and groups to come together to find solutions and work towards shared goals.

Moreover, reducing violence can create a sense of security and stability that is necessary for social and economic development. When people feel safe and secure, they are more likely to invest in their communities and pursue opportunities for education, employment, and personal growth. This can lead to increased prosperity and a higher quality of life, which can further reinforce peace and stability.

In summary, reducing violence is a crucial step towards creating a peaceful society because it can break the cycle of retaliation and retribution, facilitate dialogue and negotiation, and create a sense of security and stability that is necessary for social and economic development.

- **Promoting understanding:** Peace education promotes understanding and respect for cultural diversity. This helps to reduce prejudice and discrimination, leading to a more inclusive and harmonious society.

Promoting understanding is essential in achieving peace for several reasons:

**Reducing Misunderstandings:** Misunderstandings are a significant source of conflict between individuals, groups, and nations. By promoting understanding, people can better comprehend each other's perspectives and avoid unnecessary misunderstandings that can lead to conflict.

**Building Trust:** Understanding builds trust between people and groups, which is crucial in maintaining peaceful relationships. When people have a better understanding of each other's motivations, beliefs, and values, they are more likely to trust one another.

**Finding Common Ground:** Promoting understanding helps people identify areas of common interest, which can lead to constructive dialogue and compromise. When people understand each other's needs and concerns, they can work together to find solutions that benefit everyone.

**Reducing Prejudice and Discrimination:** By promoting understanding, people can challenge their own prejudices and biases, which can lead to more equitable and inclusive societies. When people understand the experiences and perspectives of others, they are less likely to discriminate against them based on their race, ethnicity, religion, gender, or other factors.

**Fostering Empathy:** Promoting understanding can help foster empathy, which is the ability to understand and share the feelings of others. Empathy is essential for peaceful relationships because it helps people connect with each other on a deeper level and promotes a sense of shared humanity.

In conclusion, promoting understanding is a vital step towards achieving peace. It helps reduce misunderstandings, build trust, find common ground, reduce prejudice and discrimination, and foster empathy.

- **Fostering critical thinking:** Peace education fosters critical thinking and problem-solving skills, enabling individuals to make informed decisions about conflict resolution and to create solutions that promote peace. Fostering critical thinking can be an essential tool in promoting peace because it encourages individuals to analyze information and ideas objectively, question assumptions, and consider alternative perspectives. When people engage in critical thinking, they are more likely to avoid accepting biased or incomplete information and to approach conflicts with an open mind. By encouraging critical thinking, individuals can develop a better understanding of the root causes of conflicts and the potential solutions. They can identify areas of common ground and seek out compromise rather than simply taking sides. This can lead to more constructive and peaceful dialogue between individuals or groups.

In addition, critical thinking can promote empathy and understanding. When individuals are encouraged to consider multiple perspectives, they can develop a greater appreciation for the experiences and viewpoints of others, even those with whom they disagree. This can help to break down barriers and foster a sense of community and shared humanity.

Overall, fostering critical thinking can play a crucial role in promoting peace by encouraging individuals to approach conflicts with an open mind, seek out common ground, and develop a greater appreciation for the perspectives of others.

- **Building empathy:** Peace education helps individuals to understand the perspectives of others, including those with whom they disagree or have conflicts. This can lead to increased empathy and a more compassionate approach to conflict resolution.

Empathy is the ability to understand and share the feelings of another person. Building empathy can be a powerful tool in promoting peace, as it allows individuals to better understand and relate to others, even those who may seem vastly different from themselves.

Here are some ways in which building empathy can help in peace:

**Promotes Understanding:** By understanding the perspectives, feelings, and experiences of others, we can better understand why they act the way they do, which can help prevent conflicts and misunderstandings.

**Increases Tolerance:** When we develop empathy, we become more accepting of others, even those who may have different cultural backgrounds, values, and beliefs than our own.

**Encourages Communication:** Empathy can help to create a safe and open environment for people to communicate their thoughts and feelings. This communication can lead to more peaceful solutions to conflicts.

**Fosters Cooperation:** Empathy can promote cooperation and collaboration among individuals, groups, and communities. It encourages people to work together towards a common goal, which can help to reduce tensions and build lasting peace.

**Reduces Prejudice:** Empathy can help to break down barriers and reduce prejudice by helping us to see the humanity in others. This can help to create a more inclusive and equitable society.

- **Creating a culture of peace:** Peace education helps to create a culture of peace by promoting values such as cooperation, tolerance, and respect for human rights. This can help to reduce the likelihood of violence and conflict in the future. It helps individuals to develop the skills and attitudes needed to resolve conflicts peacefully and to work towards a more harmonious society. Creating a culture of peace can greatly enhance the effectiveness of peace education efforts. A culture of peace refers to a society in which people promote and actively seek to prevent conflict, violence, and discrimination. When this culture is established, individuals are more likely to be receptive to peace education and to act in ways that are consistent with its teachings.

Here are a few ways in which creating a culture of peace can be helpful for peace education:

**It sets a positive tone:** When a culture of peace is established, people are more likely to be open-minded and willing to listen to different perspectives. This creates a positive tone that can be helpful for peace education efforts.

**It reinforces the importance of peace:** A culture of peace sends a message that peace is important and that people should strive to prevent conflict and violence. This reinforces the messages that are taught in peace education programs.

**It promotes empathy:** A culture of peace promotes empathy and understanding of others. This is an important aspect of peace education because it helps individuals to understand the perspectives and needs of others, which can reduce conflict.

**It encourages dialogue:** When people are open-minded and willing to listen to others, it creates an environment in which dialogue can thrive. This is essential for peace education because it allows individuals to discuss their differences and find common ground.

In summary, peace education is essential for creating a world that is peaceful, just, and sustainable.

### 1.3) Peace Context: Assumptions and Processes

Peace , described as a relationship between any people characterized by respect, justice and goodwill. Peace can describe calmness, serenity, and silence.

In simple language, context means the setting of an event. You can think of context as all the information you need to know to truly understand something. For example, when you watch a movie from the very start, you learn about the names of the characters, where the movie is set, and what the plot line is.

The concept of peace can have different meanings depending on the context in which it is used. At its core, peace generally refers to the absence of conflict or violence, but it can also encompass broader notions of harmony, well-being, and justice.

In the context of *international relations,* peace is often understood as the absence of war or armed conflict between nations. This can be achieved through diplomacy, negotiation, and other peaceful means of dispute resolution.

In the context of *interpersonal relationships,* peace can refer to a sense of harmony and cooperation between individuals or groups. This can involve the resolution of conflicts and the cultivation of mutual respect and understanding.

In a *broader societal context,* peace can encompass a range of social, economic, and political factors that contribute to overall well-being and stability. This might include issues such as poverty reduction, access to healthcare and education, and the promotion of democratic governance and human rights.

Overall, the concept of peace is multifaceted and can be understood in a variety of ways depending on the context in which it is used.

Peace" can refer to a variety of contexts, including:

1. **International Peace:** This refers to the absence of conflict between nations and the promotion of diplomacy and cooperation among countries. It involves negotiating and resolving conflicts peacefully, building trust and understanding among nations, and working together to address global challenges such as climate change, poverty, and human rights abuses.
2. **Inner Peace:** This refers to a state of mental and emotional calmness, serenity, and tranquility. It involves finding balance, clarity, and contentment within oneself, letting go of negative emotions and thoughts, and cultivating positive habits and practices that promote well-being and happiness.
3. **Social Peace:** This refers to a state of harmonious coexistence among individuals and groups within a society. It involves promoting respect, tolerance, and understanding among diverse communities, resolving conflicts peacefully, and creating inclusive and equitable systems that ensure equal opportunities and rights for all.
4. **Personal Peace:** This refers to a sense of inner harmony and balance that comes from living in alignment with one's values, beliefs, and purpose. It involves finding meaning and fulfillment in life, building positive relationships with oneself and others, and cultivating a sense of purpose and direction in life.

**1.3.1) Assumptions:**

The concept of peace is complex and multifaceted, and there are various underlying assumptions that inform our understanding of it. Some of the key assumptions underlying the concept of peace are:

- Conflict is a normal and inevitable part of human interaction: This assumption acknowledges that conflict is a natural aspect of human interaction and that it can arise due to differences in values, interests, and beliefs.
- Peace is not simply the absence of war: This assumption recognizes that peace is not just the absence of armed conflict but also encompasses social, economic, and political conditions that promote harmony, security, justice, and human dignity.
- Peace is a dynamic and ongoing process: This assumption acknowledges that peace is not a static state but a continuous process that requires ongoing efforts to address the root causes of conflict, prevent its recurrence, and promote sustainable development.
- Peace is a collective responsibility: This assumption recognizes that peace is not the responsibility of governments alone but requires the active participation of civil society, community leaders, and individuals at all levels of society.
- Peace is based on respect for human rights: This assumption recognizes that peace is built on a foundation of respect for human rights, including the right to life, liberty, and security of person, freedom of expression, and equality before the law.
- Peace is linked to sustainable development: This assumption recognizes that sustainable development is a key driver of peace, as poverty, inequality, and environmental degradation can fuel conflict and undermine peace.
- Peace requires dialogue and negotiation: This assumption recognizes that peace requires open and constructive dialogue, negotiation, and compromise between parties to a conflict to find mutually acceptable solutions.

Assumptions for a peace context may vary depending on the specific situation and context, but some possible general assumptions include:

**1. Willingness to engage in dialogue:** All parties involved in the conflict are willing to engage in dialogue and negotiation in good faith. Willingness to engage in dialogue is a crucial factor in promoting peace. When individuals or groups are willing to engage in dialogue with one another, they are more likely to find common ground, understand each other's perspectives, and work towards mutually beneficial solutions.

Here are some ways in which a willingness to engage in dialogue can promote peace:

- Dialogue allows people to communicate their concerns and aspirations in a non-threatening environment, leading to increased mutual understanding and trust.
- Dialogue encourages individuals or groups to work together towards common goals, promoting cooperation and collaboration.
- By engaging in dialogue, individuals or groups can address their differences and find ways to resolve conflicts peacefully.
- Dialogue can reduce the likelihood of violence by providing a platform for individuals or groups to air their grievances and work towards non-violent solutions.
- Dialogue can also promote inclusivity by creating a space for all voices to be heard and considered.

In summary, a willingness to engage in dialogue is a powerful tool for promoting peace. It helps to build trust, promote cooperation, facilitate conflict resolution, reduce violence, and foster inclusivity. By encouraging dialogue, individuals and groups can work towards creating a more peaceful and harmonious world.

**2. Trust-building:** There is a willingness to build trust between the parties, through measures such as confidence-building measures, truth and reconciliation processes, and other forms of mutual acknowledgement and understanding.

Trust-building is a crucial component of establishing and maintaining peace. When individuals and groups trust each other, they are more likely to work together, collaborate, and resolve conflicts peacefully. Good assumptions play a vital role in building trust, as they help individuals and groups approach each other with an open mind and positive intentions. Assumptions are the beliefs and expectations that individuals hold about others, and they can be either positive or negative. Good assumptions are positive beliefs that individuals hold about others, such as believing that they are honest, trustworthy, and capable. When individuals hold good assumptions about each other, they are more likely to approach each other with an open mind and give each other the benefit of the doubt. Assumptions can also help to break down stereotypes and prejudices that may exist between groups. By assuming that others are good and trustworthy, individuals may be more willing to interact with and learn from people who are different from them. This can help to build bridges between groups and foster greater understanding and empathy.

**3. Shared vision of peace:** The parties involved share a common vision of what a peaceful resolution to the conflict would look like and are willing to work towards that shared goal.A shared vision of peace can be incredibly helpful in promoting peace because it can unite individuals and communities around a common goal and provide a framework for cooperation and collaboration. When people share a vision of what peace looks like, they are more likely to work together towards that goal. This can include individuals from different backgrounds, cultures, and belief systems who may otherwise have difficulty finding common ground. By working together towards a shared vision, people can build bridges across divides and create a sense of shared purpose and identity.A shared vision of peace can also help to guide decision-making and problem-solving. When individuals and communities are guided by a clear vision of what they want to achieve, they can focus their efforts and resources towards achieving that vision. This can help to prioritize actions and initiatives, avoid distractions and disagreements, and ensure that everyone is working towards the same goal. Moreover, a shared vision of peace can promote empathy and understanding. When individuals and communities are united around a common goal, they are more likely to see each other as allies rather than adversaries. They may be more willing to listen to each other's perspectives, empathize with each other's struggles, and work together to find solutions that benefit everyone.

In short, a shared vision of peace can be incredibly powerful in promoting peace because it unites people around a common goal, provides a framework for cooperation and collaboration, guides decision-making and problem-solving, and promotes empathy and understanding.

**4. Non-violent means of conflict resolution:** All parties are committed to resolving the conflict through non-violent means, including peaceful dialogue, negotiation, mediation, and other forms of conflict resolution. Non-violent means of conflict resolution refer to methods of resolving disputes without resorting to physical force or aggression. Here are some examples:

*Negotiation* involves parties discussing the issues at hand and trying to find a mutually acceptable solution. This approach requires good communication skills, active listening, and the willingness to compromise.

*Mediation* involves a third party who is neutral and facilitates communication between the parties. The mediator helps the parties to identify common ground and work towards a resolution that satisfies all parties.

*Arbitration* involves a third party who listens to both sides of the dispute and makes a decision that is binding. The parties involved agree in advance to abide by the decision of the arbitrator.

*Collaborative problem-solving* involves working together with the other party to identify the root cause of the dispute and then jointly developing a plan to address it. This approach is effective when the parties have a long-term relationship and are willing to work together to find a solution.

*Restorative justice* involves a process that focuses on repairing the harm caused by the conflict. It involves the parties coming together to discuss the impact of their actions and developing a plan to make things right.

*Effective communication* is key to resolving conflicts. By using active listening skills, showing empathy, and expressing oneself clearly, parties can often avoid escalation of conflicts and find common ground.

These are just a few examples of non-violent means of conflict resolution. Ultimately, the goal is to find a solution that satisfies all parties and avoids the need for physical force or aggression.

**5. Respect for human rights:** All parties respect the human rights of all individuals involved in the conflict, including the right to life, freedom from torture and other forms of cruel, inhuman, or degrading treatment, and the right to freedom of thought, conscience, and religion. Respect for human rights is essential for establishing and maintaining peace in a society. When human rights are respected, individuals are able to live with dignity, freedom, and equality. This creates a stable environment in which people feel safe and secure, which is crucial for peace.

Here are some specific ways in which respect for human rights can promote peace:

*Prevents violence:* When people's human rights are respected, they are less likely to resort to violence to achieve their goals. This reduces the risk of conflict and promotes peaceful coexistence.

*Fosters social cohesion:* When people are treated equally and with respect, it promotes social cohesion and unity. This reduces the likelihood of divisions and tensions between different groups, which can lead to conflict.

*Promotes justice:* Human rights ensure that everyone is treated fairly and justly. This creates a sense of trust and confidence in the justice system, which helps to prevent conflict.

*Encourages dialogue:* Respect for human rights creates an environment where people can engage in constructive dialogue and negotiation. This helps to resolve conflicts peacefully and promotes peaceful coexistence.

Respecting human rights is a fundamental aspect of creating a peaceful society. It helps to prevent conflict and promotes social harmony, justice, and equality.

**6. Support from external actors:** External actors, such as international organizations, governments, and civil society groups, are willing to support the peace process through diplomatic efforts, funding, and other forms of support. External support can play a crucial role in promoting and sustaining peace in conflict-affected regions. Here are some ways in which external actors can contribute to peace:

- **Mediation and Negotiation:** External actors such as international organizations, neighboring states, and non-governmental organizations can play a role in mediating and negotiating peace agreements between conflicting parties. They can provide a neutral space for discussions and facilitate communication between parties to the conflict.
- **Financial Assistance:** External actors can provide financial assistance to support peacebuilding efforts. This can include funding for conflict resolution initiatives, disarmament, demobilization and reintegration programs, or other peacebuilding activities.
- **Capacity Building:** External actors can provide technical support and capacity building to strengthen the institutions and systems that promote peace, such as the justice system, security sector, and civil society organizations.
- **Humanitarian Assistance:** External actors can provide humanitarian assistance to support populations affected by conflict, including food, shelter, and medical aid. This assistance can help to reduce tensions and improve conditions for peace.
- **International Pressure:** External actors can exert international pressure on parties to the conflict to negotiate and settle their differences peacefully. This can involve sanctions, diplomatic efforts, or other forms of pressure to encourage parties to find a peaceful resolution.

External support can help to create a conducive environment for peacebuilding efforts to take place, and can provide the resources and expertise needed to promote sustainable peace.

**7.Effective governance structures:** There are effective governance structures in place that can ensure the fair and equitable distribution of resources, protect the rights of all citizens, and prevent the recurrence of conflict. Effective governance structures can play a critical role in promoting peace and stability in societies. Good governance can help to address the root causes of conflict, prevent the escalation of tensions, and promote cooperation and collaboration between different groups within society. Here are some ways in which effective governance can contribute to peace:

**Rule of law:** Effective governance ensures the rule of law is applied fairly and impartially to all citizens, regardless of their social or economic status. When people trust that they will be treated fairly and justly, they are less likely to resort to violence to address their grievances.

**Accountability:** Effective governance ensures that those in power are held accountable for their actions. This helps to prevent corruption and abuse of power, which can undermine peace and stability.

**Participation:** Effective governance allows for meaningful participation by all members of society in decision-making processes. This promotes inclusiveness and helps to address the needs and concerns of all groups, reducing the likelihood of conflict.

**Transparency:** Effective governance is transparent in its decision-making processes and actions. This promotes trust between the government and the people, and reduces the risk of misunderstandings and suspicions that can lead to conflict.

**Service delivery:** Effective governance ensures that basic services, such as healthcare, education, and infrastructure, are provided to all members of society. This reduces the risk of marginalization and exclusion, which can lead to conflict.

In summary, effective governance can help to create a peaceful and stable environment by promoting the rule of law, accountability, participation, transparency, and service delivery. By addressing the root causes of conflict and promoting cooperation and collaboration, good governance can help to build a more peaceful and inclusive society.

**1.3.2) Processes:**

***Peace processes*** can be complex and multifaceted, and there is no one-size-fits-all approach to achieving peace. However, there are some key elements that can contribute to the success of a peace process.

- **Inclusivity:** All parties involved in the conflict must be included in the peace process. This includes not only the warring parties, but also civil society groups, religious leaders, and other stakeholders who may have a role in the conflict.
- **Trust building:** Building trust among the parties is essential for the success of a peace process. This may involve confidence-building measures such as ceasefires, prisoner releases, or humanitarian aid.
- **Negotiation:** Negotiation is a key component of any peace process. Negotiations should be focused on finding common ground and identifying mutually acceptable solutions.
- **Compromise:** All parties may need to make compromises in order to reach a peace agreement. This may involve giving up some of their demands in order to achieve a broader goal of ending the conflict.
- **Implementation:** Once a peace agreement has been reached, it is important to ensure that it is implemented effectively. This may involve establishing a monitoring mechanism to ensure compliance, providing support for reconstruction and development, or addressing underlying causes of the conflict such as poverty or inequality.
- **International support:** International support can play a critical role in helping to facilitate a peace process. This may involve providing financial assistance, technical expertise, or diplomatic support.
- **Time:** Finally, it is important to recognize that achieving peace is often a long and difficult process. Patience, perseverance, and a willingness to engage in dialogue are key to ensuring the success of any peace processes.
- **Conflict analysis:** understanding the root causes and dynamics of a conflict.
- **Dialogue and negotiation:** bringing together conflicting parties to engage in constructive dialogue and find common ground.
- **Peacebuilding and reconciliation:** working towards long-term solutions that address the underlying causes of the conflict and promote healing and reconciliation.
- **Security sector reform:** ensuring that security forces are accountable and responsive to the needs of the population.
- **Transitional justice:** addressing past human rights abuses and promoting accountability, truth, and reconciliation.

It's important to note that these assumptions and processes are not mutually exclusive and often overlap in practice. Successful peacebuilding requires a comprehensive approach that takes into account the unique context and dynamics of each conflict.

**1.4) Approaches to Peace Education**

Good teaching methods and techniques make the teaching learning process

Effective,

Productive,

Interesting,

Easier, and

Successful.

Every single teaching subject requires some specific methods and techniques, which will be a perfect match for delivering content. For example:To teach Science experiments best method is the demonstration method.

To teach peace education, the following *approaches* can be practiced:

- Enquiry Method
- Value Clarification
- jurisprudential Model of Teachi ng
- Role Play
- Dramatics Play
- Yoga and Meditation
- Sports and Games
- Counseling
- Teacher Education for Peace
- Teacher As A Role Model

**l) Enquiry Method:**

Enquiry- based learning and teaching method is the right method f or motivating students to raise doubts and questions themselves. In this approach, classrooms should include space for:

Inter-cultural,

Inter-generational , and

Multi-way discussions.

Political discussions can be introduced among students with new ways of thought, instead of superficia l discussions and memorization, which suppress education. Enquiry method is appropriate for spreadingpeace culture in classrooms.Through this approach of learning:

Classroom communication is enhanced,

More socialization occurs,

Conflict free place is built.

Sharing of personal experiences and knowledge,increase students ability of

- Active listening
- Asking critical questions.

Additionally, students experience a range of perspectives and thoughts for

- Non-violent communication,
- Cultural understa nding, &
- Learn how to manage conflict.

## 2) Value Clarification

Value clarification is relatively a new method to teach peace education. The objective of this strategy is not to teach specif icvaluesbut to makethe learner

- Aware about their own personally held values and
- Do a meaningful assessment on in which ways their values stand compared to those of friends, different groups and adults in society, & to even with other societies in other times.
- It is hoped that this awareness will increase the peace culture among the learner.

Though the Value Clarification strategy includesa variety of activities,there exists a basic procedure that can befollowed while using this method:

1. Teachers should begin Peace education lessons with 'Opening up' activities, with a focus on low-risk problems and issues associated with conflict management .

2. These activities should compel students to reveal their position and opinions over the issue in an overt & explicit manner.
3. Teacher should accept student responses without judgment
4. & discourage any attempts by students to mock or challenge each other's view and outlook.
5. The students should be asked to further explain or provide a reason for holding a specific value position. This is the Clarification asP-ect of the Strategy.:.
6. Whenever possible, activities should be related to issues that have historical importance or relation with present social and political issues.

### 3) Jurisprudential Model of Teaching

The Jurisprudential model fits in the family of social interaction model. This model centered upon the idea of a society,that;

- People differ in their beliefs,priorities, and views,
- Social values legitimately conflict with one another.
- Resolving complex and controversial issues for a productive social order requires people
- Who can talk to each other &
- Negotiate their differences successfully.

Jurisprudential model of teaching is especially,an effective strategy to solve and manage major conflicts related to issues like:
Religions,
Race,
Ethnicity,
Ideology,
Economic, &
Security.

### 4) Role Play

Role-play is any activity with verbal communication, where one is speaking on behalf of others in an imaginary situation. The plus point of this method is that for a short duration, learners can 'become' anyone he/she likes.The choice is endless.

Roleplay is a simulation situation & one gets the chance to get more or less real experience. Roleplay covers many applications & can be easily done even in the classroom. This activity can be practiced using drama. After the role-play and drama is over, teacher should ask students about their feeling, views, or what they learn during role Play. It can also be used to facilitate debate about current and real issues related to various world problems.

**5)Dramatics Play**

Dramatic play refers to a type of play where one accepts role assigned to them and then act them out. It is a time when children ; Pretend to be someone or something different from themselves, dramatize actions and situations which go along with the role they have chosen to play, and breaks the walls of reality. Dramatic play may be seen as trivial by some, but,they are very useful and continue to be an important strategy in the effective teaching learning process. Whiletaking part in dramatic play,children develop many skills such as :

- Make-Believe or Pretending
- Role-Playing
- Social Skills and Interaction
- Use Of Props or Materials
- Adaptability
- Effective Communication
- Increase attention Span.
- Curiosity & imagination.

Dramatic play provides excellent opportunities to parents and teachers for developing and encouraging, peaceful culture among children from a very tender age and to give them a good head start.

**6)Yoga and Meditation**

Yoga is nothing but a bunch of various physical exercises named 'Asanas'.This >Asana helps in making an objective assessment of life's problems by controlling our:

- Anger,
- Temper,
- Awareness.

To calm nerves which in turn gives us peace. Yoga helps;

- To balance state of mind,
- Generate right thought and attitude, and

- Provide apt direction to human activities which will lead them towards the joy of fulfillment.

The first step in yoga is to calm oneself - to see things clearly. Calmness helps to generate clarity in thoughts and beliefs. Asanas such as Sukhasana, spreads a sense and feeling of general peacefulness and calmness.With peace & calm, comes understanding and clarity, which help to better coordinate a day's work. Asanas such as Vajrasana, help one to feel peace & turn our mind inwardly to have more concentration.

Meditation helps to quieten the mind and the body,thus enabling an individual to focus more on his thoughts & become more concentrated.

- Meditation improves memory,
- Create a feeling of peace and calm.
- Regular practice of mediation, make a person resourceful and intuitive.
- Teachers must encourage students to practiceyoga and meditation, itwould
- Increase their internal peace,
- Curb a culture of violence &
- Helps to maintain and move towa rds a culture of peace.

### 7) Sports and Games:

" The sound mind is a sound body."

For having good mental health, one must have good health and body development. Sports and games assist people towards peaceful change, as Helps to build strong and good character, foster spirit of cooperation and understanding, Nurture sportsmanship - fairness, courage, self-control, respect for others, and persistence.Give opportunity to feel and experience sharing & caring behavior.Provide peace to the mind, and motivating peoples to participate in games and sport improve their social behavior & cooperation mind in a long way.

### 8)Counseling

Countless people all over the world suffer from psychological issues. After any traumatic experience, one needs help;

- To mitigate the emotional and psycholog ical after-effects,
- To overcome and come out from their isolation and
- To again find purpose and meaning in their lives.

The effects and after-effects of traumatic experiencesare found most among children. Children's psychosocial well beings & responsibility to protect them from the effects of trauma have been widely recognized as a pressing issue in the humanitarian field. Some placesand causeswhich can start psychological problems among children can be;

- Home,
- Conflict,
- Congenital, or other disorders.

Counseling is used as a medium to help children to understand themselves which will lead them towards a better understanding of other aspects of their lives.

**9)Teacher Education for Peace:**

*" Education is the only defense against wars. The destiny of any nation is being shaped in the classrooms. "*Teachers are role models for students,they play a key role in modeling and shaping the destiny of future stakeholders. Therefore, teachers must be given intensive training for molding different good aspects like:

- Communication skill,
- Peace culture
- Value development, and
- Knowledge of Science and technology.
- Theteacher education programs should include components of peace education.
- The teacher education programs should include components of peace education.

The NCTE and NCERT gave suggestions to integrate the Y.llabus of P-eace education in teacher education. For promoting an effective peace culture, curricular and co-curricular activities. need to be incorporated into teacher education programs. Teacher education programs should be planned to give the right experience, to make every single teacher able to uphold their duties and responsibilities.

**1O) Teacher As A Role Model:**

A role model is a person who encourages and inspires others

- To strive for greatness,
- To live with their fullest potential,
- To see best in their potential and in themselves.

A role model can be anyone:

- Parent,
- Friend,
- Sibling,
- Teachers etc.

Teachers are generally regarded as the most influential person in any child's life. Children look to them for both guidance and advice.We learn so much from teachers, via their commitment to excellence & ability to make students realize their own personal growth.

# II

# Peace Education & Prominent Educationists

**2.1 Peace Education for National integration and International Integration**

National integration refers to the process of creating and maintaining a sense of unity and cohesion among people of diverse cultures, religions, languages, and traditions within a country. It is essential for the stability and progress of a nation. National integration involves fostering a spirit of mutual respect, understanding, and tolerance among different groups of people. It also involves promoting a sense of common identity and shared values, such as patriotism, respect for the constitution and the rule of law, and a commitment to the well-being of the nation.

Various measures can be taken to promote national integration, such as encouraging inter-cultural interactions and exchanges, promoting bilingualism or multilingualism, celebrating national festivals, promoting national symbols and icons, and providing equal opportunities and rights for all citizens regardless of their cultural or religious background. National integration is crucial for the social, economic, and political development of a country. A cohesive society with a shared vision and values can work together towards common goals, which can lead to progress and prosperity for all. National integration refers to the process of bringing together people from different cultural, linguistic, religious, and regional backgrounds to form a cohesive and unified nation. It is an important aspect of any country's development as it promotes social harmony and fosters a sense of belonging among the citizens.

India is a prime example of a country that has struggled with national integration due to its diverse population. With over 1.3 billion people, India is home to more than 2,000 ethnic groups, 22 official languages, and a wide range of religious beliefs. Despite these challenges, India has managed to maintain its national unity through various policies and initiatives.

One of the most notable initiatives is the concept of "Unity in Diversity," which recognizes and celebrates India's diversity while also emphasizing the importance of national unity. This principle is enshrined in the Indian Constitution, which provides equal rights and opportunities to all citizens regardless of their background.

Another important initiative is the promotion of national symbols such as the national flag, anthem, and emblem. These symbols serve as a unifying force and represent the shared values and aspirations of the Indian people.

Case Study :

A case study that highlights the success of national integration in India is the state of Kerala. Kerala is a small state in southern India known for its high levels of social development and communal harmony. Despite having a diverse population with a majority of Hindus, Muslims, and Christians, Kerala has managed to maintain a peaceful and inclusive society.

One of the reasons for Kerala's success is its strong social welfare policies, which have helped to reduce poverty and promote education and healthcare. This has led to a more equal distribution of resources and opportunities, which in turn has reduced social tensions and promoted a sense of solidarity among the people.

Additionally, Kerala has a long tradition of religious and cultural tolerance, with festivals and celebrations being shared and enjoyed by people of all faiths. This has created a sense of belonging and acceptance among the people, regardless of their religious background.

In conclusion, national integration is an important aspect of any country's development, particularly in diverse nations like India. Through policies and initiatives that promote social harmony and a sense of belonging, India has managed to maintain its national unity despite its diverse population. Kerala is a prime example of this success, with its strong social welfare policies and tradition of religious and cultural tolerance. Peace education is the process of teaching individuals and communities the skills, values, and attitudes necessary for peaceful and harmonious coexistence. National integration, on the other hand, refers to the process of bringing together diverse groups of people within a nation, fostering a sense of unity and solidarity.

Peace education can play a crucial role in promoting national integration in the following ways:

**Fostering understanding and empathy:** Peace education can help individuals understand the perspectives and experiences of others. By teaching about diversity, respect, and understanding, peace education can promote empathy, reduce prejudice, and encourage individuals to appreciate the value of differences.Fostering understanding and empathy can play a crucial role in building national integration by promoting a sense of unity and shared identity among individuals from diverse backgrounds. When people develop a deeper understanding of each other's experiences, perspectives, and cultures, they are more likely to feel connected and empathetic towards each other, which can lead to stronger bonds and a more cohesive society.

Here are some ways that fostering understanding and empathy can help in building national integration:

**Encouraging dialogue and communication:** By promoting open communication and dialogue, individuals from different backgrounds can share their experiences and perspectives with each other. This can help to break down barriers and create a greater sense of understanding and empathy among people from different communities.

**Reducing stereotypes and prejudice:** When people develop a deeper understanding of each other's cultures and experiences, they are less likely to rely on stereotypes and prejudices. This can help to create a more inclusive society where everyone feels valued and respected.

**Building trust and cooperation:** When people feel understood and valued, they are more likely to trust each other and work together towards common goals. This can lead to greater cooperation and collaboration, which can help to strengthen national unity and integration.

**Promoting social cohesion:** When individuals from diverse backgrounds feel connected to each other and to their country, they are more likely to feel a sense of social cohesion. This can help to promote a shared sense of identity and pride in the nation, which can contribute to a more harmonious and integrated society.

Overall, fostering understanding and empathy can play a vital role in building national integration by promoting a sense of unity, reducing stereotypes and prejudices, building trust and cooperation, and promoting social cohesion.

**Developing conflict resolution skills:** Peace education equips individuals with the necessary skills to manage conflicts effectively. These skills include active listening, negotiation, compromise, and problem-solving. By teaching individuals how to resolve conflicts peacefully, peace education can help prevent and mitigate conflicts that may arise due to differences in ethnicity, religion, culture, or language.Peace education is an approach that aims to promote the values, attitudes, and behaviors that lead to peaceful coexistence and conflict resolution. It seeks to address the root causes of conflicts by promoting empathy, understanding, and respect for diversity. Developing conflict resolution skills through peace education can be a powerful tool for building national integration. Here are some ways in which this can happen:

Increased understanding and empathy: Peace education helps individuals understand the perspectives and experiences of others. This promotes empathy and helps to reduce prejudice and stereotypes that can fuel conflicts. When people have a greater understanding of each other, they are more likely to work together and cooperate towards common goals.

Effective communication: Conflict resolution skills taught in peace education can help individuals communicate effectively in difficult situations. By learning how to express their needs and concerns without attacking or belittling others, people can resolve conflicts in a respectful and constructive way. This kind of communication can be essential for building trust and cooperation among people from diverse backgrounds.

Respect for diversity: Peace education promotes respect for diversity, which can help to reduce tensions between different groups. By celebrating the differences that make us unique, and recognizing the value of different perspectives, people can learn to work together despite their differences.

Collaboration: Conflict resolution skills taught in peace education can help individuals work collaboratively towards common goals. When people learn how to identify shared interests and work together to find solutions, they can achieve more than they would by working independently. This can be particularly powerful in contexts where there are historical or ongoing conflicts between different groups.

Reduced violence: When individuals have conflict resolution skills, they are less likely to resort to violence when faced with conflict. By learning how to resolve conflicts peacefully, individuals can reduce the likelihood of violence and promote a culture of nonviolence.

So developing conflict resolution skills through peace education can help to build national integration by promoting understanding, effective communication, respect for diversity, collaboration, and nonviolence. By investing in peace education, societies can create a more peaceful and cohesive future for all its citizens.

**Encouraging positive communication:** Peace education emphasizes the importance of positive communication, including active listening, respectful dialogue, and non-violent expression of opinions. By encouraging positive communication, peace education can help to bridge the gap between individuals and communities, promoting understanding and cooperation.

**Promoting a culture of peace:** Peace education seeks to promote a culture of peace by fostering values such as respect, tolerance, and empathy. By promoting a culture of peace, peace education can help to create a sense of shared identity and common purpose, which can contribute to national integration.

In conclusion, peace education can promote national integration by fostering understanding and empathy, developing conflict resolution skills, encouraging positive communication, and promoting a culture of peace. These efforts can help to create a more cohesive and harmonious society, where individuals and communities can thrive together.

*International Integration:*

International integration refers to the process by which countries come together to form closer economic, political, and cultural ties. This process involves the reduction of trade barriers, the creation of common institutions and policies, and the movement of people, goods, and capital across borders. The ultimate goal of international integration is to increase cooperation and interdependence among countries, which can lead to greater prosperity and peace.

There are several types of international integration, including regional integration, global integration, and functional integration. Regional integration involves the creation of trade blocs or free trade areas between neighboring countries. Examples of regional integration include the European Union (EU), the North American Free Trade Agreement (NAFTA), and the Association of Southeast Asian Nations (ASEAN).

Global integration refers to the trend towards increasing economic and political interdependence among countries around the world. This includes the growth of international trade, foreign direct investment, and the spread of technology and ideas. Global integration has been facilitated by advances in transportation, communication, and technology, which have made it easier for countries to do business with each other.

Functional integration refers to the creation of international institutions that address specific issues, such as climate change, human rights, or global health. Examples of functional integration include the United Nations (UN), the World Health Organization (WHO), and the International Criminal Court (ICC). The benefits of international integration include increased trade and investment, job creation, and economic growth. It can also lead to the sharing of knowledge, technology, and best practices among countries, which can improve productivity and innovation. International integration can also promote political stability and reduce the risk of conflict between countries. However, international integration can also have drawbacks. For example, it can lead to the loss of jobs in industries that are unable to compete with cheaper imports from other countries. It can also exacerbate income inequality and environmental degradation, as countries compete to attract investment and industry.

In conclusion, international integration is a complex and multifaceted process that involves the reduction of trade barriers, the creation of common institutions and policies, and the movement of people, goods, and capital across borders. While it has the potential to bring significant benefits, it also poses challenges that must be addressed through careful planning and cooperation among countries.

*International integration,* which refers to the increasing interconnectedness and interdependence among countries in the economic, political, social, and cultural domains, can contribute to the promotion and maintenance of peace in several ways:

**Economic interdependence:** Countries that are economically integrated are less likely to go to war with each other because of the mutual benefits that they derive from trade and investment. When countries rely on each other for goods and services, they are less likely to engage in conflict as it would disrupt the flow of trade and harm their own economies.

**Diplomatic cooperation:** International integration can facilitate diplomatic cooperation among countries through institutions such as the United Nations, the World Trade Organization, and regional organizations. These institutions provide a platform for countries to engage in dialogue, negotiate agreements, and resolve conflicts peacefully.

**Cultural exchange:** International integration promotes cultural exchange and understanding, which can help reduce mistrust and conflict among countries. When people from different countries interact and learn about each other's cultures, they are more likely to view each other as partners and allies rather than enemies.

**Collective security:** International integration can strengthen collective security arrangements, where countries come together to defend against common threats. This can include military alliances, intelligence sharing, and joint military exercises. By working together to ensure mutual security, countries can avoid conflict and maintain peace.

International integration can help reduce the likelihood of conflict among countries by promoting economic interdependence, diplomatic cooperation, cultural exchange, and collective security. By building strong relationships and interconnections, countries can work together to address shared challenges and promote peace and stability in the international system.

International integration is the process of creating bonds and connections between countries and cultures around the world. One of the most effective ways to achieve this integration is through peace education. Peace education is an approach that emphasizes the importance of promoting peace, cooperation, and mutual understanding through education.

Through peace education, individuals can learn to understand and appreciate the diversity of cultures and traditions around the world. They can also learn to recognize and respect the differences and similarities between people from different backgrounds. This understanding and appreciation can help individuals to develop empathy and compassion for others, and to develop a sense of global citizenship.

At a broader level, peace education can promote social and economic development, and can help to reduce conflict and violence in societies. By providing individuals with the skills and knowledge to resolve conflicts peacefully, peace education can help to prevent conflicts from escalating into violence. It can also help to build a culture of peace and non-violence, which can lead to greater stability and prosperity in societies.

International integration through peace education can be achieved in a number of ways. One approach is to incorporate peace education into school curricula, from primary school through university. This can help to ensure that young people are exposed to the principles of peace and cooperation from an early age. Peace education can also be promoted through community organizations, cultural exchanges, and other forms of cross-cultural interaction. Another approach to promoting international integration through peace education is to support international initiatives and programs that promote peace and cooperation. These may include international conferences, seminars, and workshops, as well as international exchange programs for educators and students. By participating in these initiatives, individuals can learn about the experiences and perspectives of people from other cultures, and can develop the skills and knowledge to work effectively with people from diverse backgrounds.

In conclusion, international integration through peace education is a powerful way to promote understanding, cooperation, and mutual respect between cultures and countries around the world. By promoting peace education, individuals can learn to appreciate the diversity of cultures and traditions, develop empathy and compassion for others, and build a culture of peace and non-violence. Ultimately, this can lead to greater stability, prosperity, and cooperation in societies around the world. Peace education is a form of education that aims to foster a culture of peace and nonviolence by providing learners with the knowledge, skills, and attitudes necessary for them to become active, responsible, and engaged global citizens. Peace education is essential in promoting international integration, as it helps individuals to understand and appreciate the diversity of cultures, values, and beliefs that exist in different parts of the world. In this case study, we will explore how peace education can be used for international integration.

*Case Study:*

In 2015, the United Nations launched the Sustainable Development Goals (SDGs), a set of 17 goals aimed at creating a more sustainable and equitable world by 2030. One of the SDGs is "Quality Education," which includes a target to promote "global citizenship education" and "education for sustainable development." The goal of this target is to equip learners with the knowledge, skills, and values needed to live and work in a world that is increasingly interconnected and interdependent.

In response to this target, the International School of Geneva (ISG) launched a peace education program in 2016. The program, known as the "Peace and Conflict Studies" program, is designed to provide students with a deep understanding of the root causes of conflict and violence, and the skills and attitudes needed to create a more peaceful and just world.

The program is based on four key pillars:

1. Understanding Conflict and Violence: Students learn about the different forms of conflict and violence that exist in the world, including interpersonal, intergroup, and international conflicts. They also learn about the root causes of these conflicts, including poverty, inequality, and discrimination.
2. Building Peaceful Relationships: Students learn how to build positive and respectful relationships with others, even in the face of conflict or disagreement. They also learn how to communicate effectively and how to resolve conflicts peacefully.
3. Advocacy and Activism: Students learn how to be advocates for peace and justice in their local and global communities. They are encouraged to take action on issues that matter to them, such as human rights, environmental sustainability, and social justice.
4. Global Citizenship: Students learn about the interconnectedness of the world and the importance of understanding and appreciating different cultures, values, and beliefs. They are encouraged to be active and responsible global citizens, who contribute to making the world a more peaceful and just place. The program has been very successful in promoting international integration. Students who have completed the program have reported a greater understanding and appreciation of different cultures and perspectives. They have also reported feeling more empowered to take action on issues that matter to them, both locally and globally. *Conclusion:* Peace education is an essential tool for promoting international integration. By providing learners with the knowledge, skills, and attitudes needed to become active and responsible global citizens, peace education can help to create a more peaceful and just world. The success of the Peace and Conflict Studies program at the International School of Geneva demonstrates the power of peace education to promote international integration and create a more sustainable and equitable world.

**2.2) Peace Education propagated by M.K. Gandhi:**

Mahatma Gandhi, one of the most influential figures in the history of India and a leader of the Indian independence movement, was a staunch advocate of peace and nonviolence. He strongly believed in the transformative power of peace education and actively propagated its principles throughout his life. Gandhi believed that peace should not be viewed merely as the absence of violence but as a proactive and constructive approach to resolving conflicts and promoting harmony. He recognized that achieving lasting peace requires addressing the underlying causes of violence and injustice, and he saw education as a key tool in this process.He emphasized the importance of education in developing individuals who are committed to peace, justice, and nonviolence. He believed that education should go beyond imparting academic knowledge and should strive to cultivate virtues such as compassion, empathy, understanding, and respect for all individuals. Gandhi believed that education should be holistic, focusing on the development of the mind, body, and spirit.

One of the central concepts Gandhi promoted in peace education was the principle of "Satyagraha," which means "truth-force" or "soul-force." Satyagraha is a nonviolent method of resistance and social change that Gandhi employed during the Indian independence movement. He believed that by adhering to truth and nonviolence, individuals can confront injustice and transform society peacefully.

Gandhi advocated for incorporating peace education in schools and communities. He stressed the need to teach conflict resolution skills, promote interfaith dialogue, and foster understanding between different communities. He believed that peace education should be accessible to all, regardless of their social or economic background. Furthermore, Gandhi recognized the importance of personal transformation in the pursuit of peace. He believed that individuals should strive to embody the principles they advocate and be the change they want to see in the world. Gandhi famously said, "You must be the change you wish to see in the world."

Gandhi's teachings on peace education continue to inspire people around the world. His emphasis on nonviolence, truth, and compassion as essential elements of education and social change has had a profound impact on peace movements and the field of conflict resolution. His philosophy serves as a guiding light for those who seek to promote peace and justice through education and nonviolent means.

Gandhi ji was a strong advocate for peace education and believed that education was a powerful tool for promoting nonviolence, tolerance, and understanding among people from different backgrounds. He believed that peace education was essential for achieving social and political change, and that it could help to prevent conflict and violence.

Gandhi ji's approach to peace education emphasized the importance of understanding the root causes of violence and conflict, and addressing them through nonviolent means. He believed that this required a deep understanding of human nature and a commitment to promoting compassion, empathy, and understanding.

One of the key principles of Gandhi ji's approach to peace education was the idea of "satyagraha," or nonviolent resistance. He believed that nonviolent resistance was a powerful tool for promoting social change and addressing injustice, and that it could help to create a more peaceful and just society.

In addition to promoting nonviolence and nonviolent resistance, Gandhi ji also emphasized the importance of tolerance and understanding. He believed that people from different backgrounds and with different beliefs could learn to live together in peace and harmony, but that this required a willingness to listen and understand each other's perspectives.

Overall, Gandhi ji's approach to peace education emphasized the importance of promoting nonviolence, tolerance, and understanding, and of using education as a tool for promoting social and political change. His teachings continue to inspire peace activists and educators around the world today.

Gandhi's approach to teaching peace education was rooted in his belief in experiential learning and practical application of principles. Here are some of the methods he employed:

Lead by Example: Gandhi believed that teachers should embody the values they seek to instill in their students. He emphasized the importance of personal transformation and encouraged educators to live a life of nonviolence, truth, and compassion. By being a role model, teachers could inspire their students to emulate these values in their own lives.

Dialogue and Discussion: Gandhi encouraged open dialogue and discussion as a means to promote understanding and resolve conflicts. He believed in creating a safe and inclusive space for students to express their thoughts, concerns, and perspectives. Through meaningful conversations, students could develop empathy, respect diverse viewpoints, and learn the art of peaceful communication.

Nonviolent Conflict Resolution: Gandhi emphasized the importance of teaching students skills and strategies for resolving conflicts nonviolently. He believed in empowering individuals to address disputes through peaceful means, such as dialogue, negotiation, mediation, and compromise. Students were encouraged to analyze conflicts from multiple perspectives and seek win-win solutions.

Reflection and Self-Awareness: Gandhi believed in the power of self-reflection and self-awareness as tools for personal growth and transformation. Students were encouraged to introspect and critically examine their own actions, thoughts, and biases. This process of self-reflection helped them identify areas for improvement, develop empathy, and become more conscious of the impact of their actions on others.

Service and Social Action: Gandhi emphasized the importance of taking action to create positive change in society. He believed in the value of service to others and encouraged students to actively engage in community service and social justice initiatives. Through these hands-on experiences, students could understand the realities of social issues and develop a sense of responsibility and compassion towards others.

Practical Exercises: Gandhi employed practical exercises to reinforce the principles of peace education. These exercises included activities such as role-playing, simulations, and group projects aimed at fostering teamwork, empathy, and conflict resolution skills. By engaging in these experiential learning opportunities, students could internalize the values of peace and nonviolence.

Overall, Gandhi's teaching methods for peace education emphasized a holistic approach that combined personal transformation, dialogue, experiential learning, and practical application. By incorporating these methods, he aimed to cultivate individuals who not only possessed knowledge but also actively practiced peace, nonviolence, and social justice in their lives.

### 2.2.1) Peace Education propagated by Sri Aurobindo Ghosh :

Sri Aurobindo Ghosh, also known as Sri Aurobindo, was a philosopher, yogi, and poet who lived in India during the 20th century. He was a strong advocate of peace and believed that education was one of the most powerful tools for promoting peace and harmony in the world.

Aurobindo Ghosh's concept of peace education was based on the idea that true peace can only be achieved through inner transformation ""Inner transformation relates to various aspects of human existence and interactions such as consciousness, mindsets, values, worldviews, beliefs, spirituality and human–nature connectedness"". He believed that education should help individuals develop a deep understanding of their own inner nature and cultivate qualities such as love, compassion, and empathy. In his view, this would enable individuals to live in harmony with themselves and with others, promoting peace both within themselves and in the wider world.

Aurobindo Ghosh's approach to peace education also emphasized the importance of holistic learning. He believed that education should encompass not only intellectual development but also emotional, physical, and spiritual growth. He believed that a balanced and integrated approach to education could help individuals develop a more complete and harmonious understanding of themselves and the world around them, leading to greater peace and well-being.

In summary, Aurobindo Ghosh's concept of peace education emphasized the importance of inner transformation, holistic learning, and the cultivation of qualities such as love, compassion, and empathy. He believed that education could be a powerful tool for promoting peace and harmony in the world, and his ideas continue to inspire educators and peace advocates today.

*Sri Aurobindo Ghosh* was a philosopher, poet, and spiritual leader who lived in India during the 20th century. He was a prominent figure in the Indian independence movement and later became a major spiritual leader and advocate of integral yoga.

Aurobindo Ghosh's ideology was rooted in his belief in the inherent divinity of human beings and his vision of a divine transformation of the world. He believed that human evolution was not limited to physical or intellectual development but also included a spiritual evolution, which he called the "Supramental transformation." In his view, this transformation would involve a radical shift in human consciousness, enabling individuals to transcend the limitations of the ego and experience a new level of unity and harmony with all beings.

Aurobindo Ghosh's ideology also emphasized the importance of integral yoga, a spiritual practice that seeks to integrate all aspects of human nature - physical, emotional, intellectual, and spiritual - in pursuit of self-realization and the realization of a higher, divine consciousness. He believed that integral yoga could help individuals achieve a higher state of consciousness and experience a deeper sense of purpose, meaning, and fulfillment in life.

In addition to his spiritual teachings, Aurobindo Ghosh was also a political thinker and activist, who believed that political freedom was a necessary condition for spiritual and social progress. He was a strong advocate of Indian independence and played a prominent role in the Indian nationalist movement.

Aurobindo Ghosh's ideology was a synthesis of spirituality, philosophy, and politics, which emphasized the importance of human evolution, integral yoga, and the pursuit of divine consciousness for the betterment of humanity and the world.

Aurobindo Ghosh was a strong advocate of peace and believed that education was a powerful tool for promoting peace and harmony in the world. He believed that true peace could only be achieved through inner transformation and that education should help individuals develop a deep understanding of their own inner nature and cultivate qualities such as love, compassion, and empathy.

Aurobindo Ghosh's views on peace education were based on the idea that education should be holistic and encompass not only intellectual development but also emotional, physical, and spiritual growth. He believed that a balanced and integrated approach to education could help individuals develop a more complete and harmonious understanding of themselves and the world around them, leading to greater peace and well-being.

Aurobindo Ghosh emphasized the importance of developing a sense of unity and interconnectedness among individuals and promoting a culture of mutual respect, tolerance, and non-violence. He believed that education should cultivate in individuals a deep appreciation for diversity and encourage them to embrace differences and celebrate the richness of human experience.

Aurobindo Ghosh also believed that education should encourage individuals to take responsibility for their own personal growth and development and inspire them to work for the greater good of society. He believed that education should help individuals develop a sense of purpose and meaning in life, which would enable them to lead fulfilling and productive lives and make a positive contribution to the world.

In summary, Aurobindo Ghosh's views on peace education emphasized the importance of inner transformation, holistic learning, and the cultivation of qualities such as love, compassion, and empathy. He believed that education could be a powerful tool for promoting peace and harmony in the world, and his ideas continue to inspire educators and peace advocates today.

Aurobindo Ghosh's methods of teaching peace education were based on the principles of integral education, which he believed should encompass not only intellectual development but also emotional, physical, and spiritual growth. He believed that a balanced and integrated approach to education could help individuals develop a more complete and harmonious understanding of themselves and the world around them, leading to greater peace and well-being.

Here are some of the methods Aurobindo Ghosh proposed for teaching peace education:

Encouraging self-reflection: Aurobindo Ghosh believed that individuals should be encouraged to reflect on their own inner nature and cultivate qualities such as love, compassion, and empathy. This can be achieved through activities such as journaling, meditation, and contemplation.

Cultivating intercultural understanding: Aurobindo Ghosh emphasized the importance of developing a sense of unity and interconnectedness among individuals and promoting a culture of mutual respect, tolerance, and non-violence. This can be achieved through activities such as intercultural exchange programs, cultural festivals, and diversity workshops.

Fostering critical thinking: Aurobindo Ghosh believed that education should encourage individuals to think critically and independently, and to question assumptions and beliefs that lead to conflict and division. This can be achieved through activities such as debate, group discussion, and analysis of current events.

Promoting mindfulness and stress reduction: Aurobindo Ghosh believed that education should help individuals develop a sense of inner peace and well-being, which can in turn promote peaceful interactions with others. This can be achieved through activities such as yoga, meditation, and mindfulness practices.

Encouraging social action: Aurobindo Ghosh believed that education should inspire individuals to work for the greater good of society and to take responsibility for creating positive change in the world. This can be achieved through activities such as community service, activism, and social entrepreneurship.

Overall, Aurobindo Ghosh's methods of teaching peace education were designed to cultivate a deep sense of personal and social responsibility, promote intercultural understanding and respect, and foster a more peaceful and harmonious world.

### 2.2.2) Peace Education propagated by Swami Vivekananda:

Swami Vivekananda was a prominent Indian philosopher and spiritual leader of the late 19th and early 20th centuries. He emphasized the importance of education as a means of empowering individuals and societies, and his ideas on education continue to inspire people around the world.

According to Swami Vivekananda, education should not just be about memorizing facts and figures. Rather, it should be a holistic process that helps individuals develop their physical, intellectual, emotional, and spiritual potential.

One of his famous quotes on education is, "Education is not the amount of information that is put into your brain and runs riot there, undigested all your life. We must have life-building, man-making, character-making assimilation of ideas."

He believed that education should focus on developing one's character and values, as well as their intellect. He believed that the aim of education should be to help individuals become self-reliant, confident, and socially responsible citizens.

Swami Vivekananda also emphasized the importance of practical education that teaches skills relevant to the real world. He believed that education should not just be theoretical, but should also be applied in practice to solve real-world problems.

In conclusion, Swami Vivekananda believed that education should be a holistic process that develops the physical, intellectual, emotional, and spiritual potential of individuals. He emphasized the importance of practical education that teaches skills relevant to the real world, and the development of character and values alongside intellectual growth.

**Peace Education by Swami Vivekananda:**

Swami Vivekananda believed that education should not only focus on intellectual development but also on spiritual and moral development. He emphasized the importance of peace education, which he believed could help individuals and societies cultivate inner peace and foster peaceful relationships with others.

According to Swami Vivekananda, peace education should be centered around the development of spiritual and moral values such as love, compassion, and non-violence. He believed that these values could help individuals overcome negative emotions such as anger and hatred, which are often the cause of conflicts and violence.

In his famous speech at the World's Parliament of Religions in 1893, Swami Vivekananda said, "I fervently hope that the bell that tolled this morning in honor of this convention may be the death-knell of all fanaticism, of all persecutions with the sword or with the pen, and of all uncharitable feelings between persons wending their way to the same goal."

Swami Vivekananda believed that education can be a powerful tool for promoting peace and social harmony. He believed that by teaching individuals the values of non-violence, mutual respect, and compassion, we can create a more peaceful and just society.

Swami Vivekananda believed that peace education was an essential component of holistic education. He emphasized the importance of spiritual and moral values such as love, compassion, and non-violence, which can help individuals and societies cultivate inner peace and promote social harmony.

Swami Vivekananda's teaching methods for peace education were rooted in the belief that education should be holistic, practical, and experiential. He believed that peace education should not only teach the principles of peace but also provide opportunities for individuals to practice them in their daily lives.

Here are some of the teaching methods of peace education that Swami Vivekananda emphasized:

Meditation and reflection: Swami Vivekananda believed that meditation and self-reflection were powerful tools for promoting inner peace and self-awareness. He encouraged individuals to take time for meditation and self-reflection as part of their daily routine.

Active learning: Swami Vivekananda believed in the importance of active learning, where individuals learn through experience and practice. He believed that peace education should provide opportunities for individuals to practice peace-building skills such as conflict resolution, empathy, and non-violent communication.

Service learning: Swami Vivekananda emphasized the importance of service to others as a means of promoting peace and social harmony. He believed that peace education should provide opportunities for individuals to engage in community service and social action projects.

Cultural exchange: Swami Vivekananda believed in the power of cultural exchange as a means of promoting understanding and mutual respect among different communities. He encouraged individuals to engage in cultural exchange programs that promote intercultural dialogue and understanding.

Role modeling: Swami Vivekananda believed that teachers should model the principles of peace and non-violence in their own behavior. He emphasized the importance of teachers serving as positive role models for their students.

In conclusion, Swami Vivekananda's teaching methods for peace education were centered around active learning, service learning, cultural exchange, and role modeling. He believed that education should be holistic, practical, and experiential, providing opportunities for individuals to practice the principles of peace in their daily lives.

**2.3) NCF 2005 recommendations on Peace Education:**

NCF 2005 stands for the National Curriculum Framework (NCF) 2005, which is an educational framework developed by the National Council of Educational Research and Training (NCERT) in India. The framework was first introduced in 2005 and revised in 2019.

The NCF 2005 provides guidelines for the development of school curricula and teaching practices in India. It emphasizes the need for a learner-centered approach to education, where the focus is on the holistic development of the child, rather than just academic performance. The framework recognizes the diversity of learners and encourages the use of a variety of teaching methods to cater to different learning styles.

The NCF 2005 also highlights the importance of promoting values such as democracy, secularism, social justice, and environmental sustainability through the school curriculum. It encourages the use of innovative and creative teaching practices that can help students develop critical thinking, problem-solving, and decision-making skills.

Overall, the NCF 2005 has had a significant impact on the Indian education system, as it has helped to promote a more inclusive and student-centered approach to teaching and learning.

The National Curriculum Framework (NCF) 2005 in India emphasizes the need to provide a holistic education that goes beyond academic knowledge and includes the social, emotional, and ethical development of the learners. It recognizes the importance of peace education in promoting a culture of peace and non-violence in society.

The following are some of the key principles and objectives of the NCF that can guide the teaching of peace education:

Child-Centered Approach: Peace education should be designed keeping in mind the diverse learning styles and abilities of learners. Teachers should adopt a child-centered approach that encourages learners to actively participate in the learning process.

Holistic Education: Peace education should focus on the social, emotional, and ethical development of learners in addition to their academic knowledge.

Inclusiveness: Peace education should be inclusive and address the needs of learners from diverse backgrounds, including those from marginalized communities.Inclusive education is a type of education where education is provided to all the students irrespective of their caste, religion, race, color, gender, and disabilities

Constructivist Approach: Peace education should adopt a constructivist approach that encourages learners to actively construct their own understanding of peace and non-violence.

Integration of Knowledge: Peace education should promote the integration of knowledge across subject areas, including history, social science, and literature.

Value-Based Education: Peace education should be grounded in values such as empathy, compassion, and respect for diversity.

Active Learning: Peace education should emphasize active learning through collaborative activities, discussions, and projects.

Reflection and Self-Evaluation: Peace education should encourage learners to reflect on their own attitudes and behaviors towards peace and non-violence and to evaluate their own progress in developing these values.

By incorporating these principles and objectives, teachers can create a learning environment that promotes peace and non-violence and prepares learners to become responsible and engaged citizens who can contribute to a more peaceful and just society.

The National Curriculum Framework (NCF) 2005 recommends peace education as an essential part of school education. According to the NCF, peace education should be taught as a part of the curriculum in schools to foster values of peace, nonviolence, cooperation, and harmony among students.

The NCF 2005 emphasizes that peace education should be integrated into various subjects and activities, including social studies, history, literature, arts, and cultural programs. The framework also suggests that peace education should be taught in a way that connects with students' daily experiences and encourages critical thinking, creativity, and empathy.

The NCF 2005 also highlights the importance of peace education in building a democratic and pluralistic society. It recommends that peace education should enable students to understand the principles of democracy, social justice, human rights, and conflict resolution.

In summary, the NCF 2005 recommends that peace education should be an integral part of school education to promote values of peace and harmony among students and prepare them to be responsible and active citizens of a democratic and pluralistic society.

**The objectives of the NCF are to:**

- Promote quality education for all learners.
- Encourage the development of critical thinking and creativity among learners.
- Provide a flexible and adaptable curriculum that takes into account the needs of learners.
- Foster inclusive education that promotes equity and social justice.
- Develop a culture of learning that values lifelong learning and continuous improvement.
- Promote the integration of technology in education to enhance learning experiences.

# III
# Human Rights & Fundamental Rights

**3.1) Historical background of human rights.**

The history of human rights covers thousands of years and draws upon religious, cultural, philosophical and legal developments throughout the recorded history. It seems that the concept of human rights is as old as the civilization. This is evident from the fact that almost at all stages of mankind there have been a human rights documents in one form or the other in existence. Several ancient documents and later religious and philosophies included a variety of concepts that may be considered to be human rights. Notable among such documents are the Edicts of Ashoka issued by Ashoka the Great of India between 272-231 BC . However, the idea for the protection of human rights grew after the tragic experiences of the two world wars. Prior to the world war, there was not much codification done either at the national or the international levels for the protection and implementation of human rights.

This topic seeks to analyse the concept and approaches of human rights and its development even before the Greek times. In this regard, the period has been classified as pre world wars and post war eras. The latter has been further divided into normative foundation, institution building and stage of implementation. Several important documents like Magna Carta, French Declaration of the Rights of Man, UDHR, ICCPR etc. and a brief discussion of various approaches to human rights have been mentioned.

The concept of human rights refers to the fundamental rights and freedoms that every individual is inherently entitled to, regardless of their nationality, race, gender, religion, or any other distinguishing characteristic. These rights are considered universal, inalienable, and indivisible, meaning they apply to all human beings equally and cannot be taken away or separated from a person. Human rights refer to the "basic rights and freedoms to which all humans are entitled." Examples of rights and freedoms which have come to be commonly thought of as human rights include civil and political rights, such as the right to life and liberty, freedom of expression, and equality before the law; and social, cultural and economic rights, including the right to participate in culture, the right to food, the right to work, and the right to education. "A human right is a universal moral right, something which all men, everywhere, at all times ought to have, something of which no one may be deprived without a grave affront to justice, something which is owing to every human simply because he is human." Human rights are inalienable: you cannot lose these rights any more than you can cease being a human being. Human rights are indivisible: you cannot be denied a right because it is "less important" or "non-essential." Human rights are interdependent: all human rights are part of a complementary framework. For example, your ability to participate in your government is directly affected by your right to express yourself, to get an education, and even to obtain the necessities of life.

Human rights are based on the principle that all individuals possess inherent dignity and worth, and they should be treated with respect, fairness, and equality. The concept emerged as a response to historical injustices and abuses of power, with the aim of promoting and protecting the well-being and autonomy of individuals and societies.

The modern understanding of human rights is primarily derived from the Universal Declaration of Human Rights (UDHR), adopted by the United Nations General Assembly in 1948. The UDHR outlines a broad range of civil, political, economic, social, and cultural rights that are considered fundamental for all individuals. These include the right to life, liberty, and security; freedom of thought, expression, and religion; the right to education, healthcare, and work; and freedom from discrimination, torture, and slavery, among others. Human rights are protected through various mechanisms, including national and international legal frameworks, institutions, and advocacy efforts. Many countries have incorporated human rights principles into their constitutional laws, and international treaties and conventions exist to promote and enforce human rights standards globally. The concept of human rights is based on the belief that every individual has inherent value and deserves to be treated with dignity, equality, and fairness. It serves as a guide for governments, organizations, and individuals in their interactions and responsibilities towards one another, with the goal of creating a just and inclusive society for all. Human rights" are rights inherent to all human beings, regardless of our nationality, residence, sex, sexual orientation and gender identity, national or ethnic origin, color, religion, language or any other status. We are all equally entitled to our human rights without discrimination. This is the modern concept of our fundamental rights but it was not always this way. The belief that everyone, by virtue of her or his humanity, is entitled to certain human rights is fairly new and is something stemming from an evolution of the consideration of human dignity over the last centuries. Its roots lie in earlier tradition and documents of many cultures.

The origins of Human Rights are ideally pinpointed to the year 539 BC. When the troops of Cyrus the Great conquered Babylon. Cyrus freed the slaves, declared that all people had the right to choose their own religion, and established racial equality. These and other principles were recorded on a baked-clay cylinder known as the Cyrus Cylinder, whose provisions served as inspiration for the first four Articles of the Universal Declaration of Human Rights.

Originally, people had rights only because of their membership in a group, such as a family. Then, in 539 BC, Cyrus the Great, after conquering the city of Babylon, did something totally unexpected—he freed all slaves to return home. Moreover, he declared people should choose their own religion. The Cyrus Cylinder, a clay tablet containing his statements, is the first human rights declaration in history. The idea of human rights spread quickly to India, Greece and eventually Rome. The most important advances since then have included:

*1215: The Magna Carta—gave people new rights and made the king subject to the law.*

*1628: The Petition of Right—set out the rights of the people.*

*1776: The United States Declaration of Independence—proclaimed the right to life, liberty and the pursuit of happiness.*

*1789: The Declaration of the Rights of Man and of the Citizen—a document of France, stating that all citizens are equal under the law.*

*1948: The Universal Declaration of Human Rights—the first document listing the 30 rights to which everyone is entitled.*

The concept of human rights has evolved over centuries and is deeply rooted in the history of human civilization. While the idea of human rights as we understand them today may be a relatively recent development, the foundations of human rights can be traced back to ancient civilizations and philosophical traditions.

**Ancient Civilizations:** Many ancient civilizations, such as the Mesopotamian, Egyptian, and Indus Valley civilizations, had legal codes that recognized certain rights and protections for individuals. For example, the Code of Hammurabi, created in ancient Babylon (circa 1754 BCE), established laws that emphasized the principle of justice and included provisions for the protection of personal liberties and property.

**Classical Greece and Rome:** Ancient Greece and Rome made significant contributions to the development of human rights through the ideas of philosophers and statesmen. Greek philosophers like Socrates, Plato, and Aristotle contemplated the nature of justice, equality, and individual freedom. In Rome, the concept of natural law emerged, which posited that certain rights were inherent to all human beings by virtue of their humanity.

**Magna Carta:** Signed in 1215 in England, the Magna Carta is considered a landmark document in the history of human rights. It was a feudal charter that limited the powers of the monarchy and established the principle that even kings were subject to the law. While it primarily protected the rights of the nobility, it laid the foundation for the idea of legal rights and due process.The English Magna Carta of 1215 granted by King John is very much significant in the development of human rights. The overreaching theme of Magna Carta was protection against arbitrary acts by the King. Land and Property could no longer be seized, judges had to know and respect laws, taxes could not be imposed without common council. The Carta also introduced the concept of jury trial in Clause 39, which protect against arbitrary arrest and imprisonment. Thus, Carta set forth the principle that the power of king was not absolute. The Carta was later converted to Bill of Rights in 1689.

**Enlightenment Era:** The Enlightenment period of the 17th and 18th centuries played a pivotal role in shaping modern conceptions of human rights. Enlightenment thinkers such as John Locke, Thomas Hobbes, and Jean-Jacques Rousseau put forth ideas about individual rights, social contracts, and the inherent dignity of human beings. These ideas challenged the notion of absolute monarchy and influenced the American and French Revolutions.

**American Revolution and Declaration of Independence:** The American Revolution, which culminated in the Declaration of Independence in 1776, proclaimed the natural rights of individuals, including "life, liberty, and the pursuit of happiness." This influential document articulated the idea that governments should exist to protect and uphold the rights of individuals.

**French Revolution and Declaration of the Rights of Man and of the Citizen:** The French Revolution, starting in 1789, led to the adoption of the Declaration of the Rights of Man and of the Citizen in 1789. This document emphasized the principles of liberty, equality, and fraternity and became a cornerstone of modern human rights. It recognized the equal rights of all individuals and the concept of popular sovereignty.

**International Human Rights Framework:** The modern international human rights framework emerged after World War II, in response to the atrocities committed during the war. The Universal Declaration of Human Rights (UDHR), adopted by the United Nations General Assembly in 1948, is a key document in this regard. It sets out a comprehensive range of civil, political, economic, social, and cultural rights that are universally applicable to all human beings.

Since the adoption of the UDHR, human rights have been further codified and protected through various international treaties, such as the International Covenant on Civil and Political Rights (ICCPR) and the International Covenant on Economic, Social and Cultural Rights (ICESCR). These treaties, along with regional human rights instruments, have formed the basis for the promotion and protection of human rights worldwide.

It's important to note that the realization of human rights is an ongoing process, and there are still challenges and struggles to ensure the full enjoyment of human rights for all individuals globally.

**Universal Declaration of Human Rights (UDHR):** The UDHR, adopted by the United Nations General Assembly in 1948, is a milestone document that sets out the fundamental human rights to be universally protected. It defines human rights as inherent to all individuals, without distinction, and encompasses civil, political, economic, social, and cultural rights.

**International Covenant on Civil and Political Rights (ICCPR):** The ICCPR is an international treaty adopted by the United Nations General Assembly in 1966. It focuses on civil and political rights, such as the right to life, freedom of speech, religion, and assembly, and the right to a fair trial.

**International Covenant on Economic, Social and Cultural Rights (ICESCR):** Also adopted in 1966, the ICESCR is another international treaty that emphasizes economic, social, and cultural rights. It recognizes rights such as the right to work, education, healthcare, social security, and an adequate standard of living.

**European Convention on Human Rights (ECHR):** The ECHR is a regional human rights treaty established by the Council of Europe in 1950. It protects a wide range of civil and political rights and establishes a European Court of Human Rights to ensure compliance with the convention.

**African Charter on Human and Peoples' Rights:** Adopted in 1981 by the Organization of African Unity (now African Union), this regional treaty promotes and protects human rights in Africa. It recognizes civil, political, economic, social, and cultural rights, as well as the collective rights of peoples.

**Human Rights Act (HRA):** The Human Rights Act is a domestic law enacted by several countries, including the United Kingdom. It incorporates the rights and freedoms protected by the European Convention on Human Rights into domestic law, allowing individuals to bring human rights claims in national courts.

These definitions and legal instruments provide frameworks for understanding and protecting human rights at the international and regional levels. They outline the specific rights and freedoms that individuals are entitled to and serve as a guide for governments and institutions to ensure respect for human dignity, equality, and justice.

Human rights are fundamental to the stability and development of countries all around the world. Great emphasis has been placed on international conventions and their implementation in order to ensure adherence to a universal standard of acceptability. With the advent of globalization and the introduction of new technology, these principles gain importance not only in protecting human beings from the ill-effects of change but also in ensuring that all are allowed a share of the benefits.

The impact of several changes in the world today on human rights has been both negative and positive. In particular, the risks posed by advancements in science and technology may severely hinder the implementation of human rights if not handled carefully. In the field of biotechnology and medicine especially there is strong need for human rights to be absorbed into ethical codes and for all professionals to ensure that basic human dignity is protected under all circumstances. For instance, with the possibility of transplanting organs from both the living and dead, a number of issues arise such as consent to donation, the definition of death to prevent premature harvesting, an equal chance at transplantation etc. Genetic engineering also brings with it the dangers of gene mutation and all the problems associated with cloning. In order to deal with these issues, the Convention for the Protection of Human Rights and Dignity of the Human Being with Regard to the Application and Medicine puts the welfare of the human being above society or science

### 3.2) Fundamental rights as included in Indian Constitution:

The concept of fundamental rights refers to a set of basic human rights that are considered essential for the protection and well-being of individuals. These rights are typically enshrined in a country's constitution or international declarations and treaties. Fundamental rights are often considered to be inherent to all individuals, regardless of their nationality, race, gender, religion, or other characteristics.

The purpose of fundamental rights is to safeguard individual freedoms and ensure that individuals are protected from any undue interference or violation by the state or other entities. They are designed to establish a framework for a just and equitable society, promoting human dignity, equality, and justice.

The specific rights included in the concept of fundamental rights can vary from one country to another, but some commonly recognized fundamental rights include:

*Right to life:* The right to life is the most fundamental of all rights, protecting individuals from arbitrary deprivation of life.

Right to liberty and security: This includes the right to personal freedom, protection against arbitrary arrest or detention, and the right to a fair trial.

Right to equality: This encompasses the principle of non-discrimination and ensures equal treatment and opportunities for all individuals, irrespective of their characteristics.

Right to freedom of expression: This right protects individuals' freedom to express their opinions, beliefs, and ideas without censorship or fear of retaliation.

Right to privacy: This right safeguards individuals' privacy and personal information, protecting them from unwarranted surveillance or intrusion into their private lives.

Right to freedom of religion: This includes the freedom to practice and express one's religion or beliefs, as well as the freedom to change one's religion or belief system.

Right to education: This ensures that individuals have access to quality education, promoting intellectual and personal development.

Right to work and fair conditions of employment: This includes the right to work, fair wages, safe working conditions, and the freedom to join trade unions.

Right to health: This encompasses the right to access healthcare services, including medical care, sanitation, and a healthy environment.

Right to freedom of assembly and association: This protects individuals' right to peacefully assemble, form associations, and engage in collective activities.

It's important to note that the list above is not exhaustive, and the specific rights recognized as fundamental may vary depending on the legal and cultural context. Fundamental rights serve as a safeguard against potential abuses of power and aim to ensure the protection and well-being of individuals within a society.

The concept of fundamental rights in the Indian Constitution drew inspiration from various sources and legal traditions. The framers of the Indian Constitution, led by Dr. B.R. Ambedkar and the Constituent Assembly, took inspiration from both national and international sources while formulating the fundamental rights provisions. Some of the key sources from which India borrowed the concept of fundamental rights include:

**Universal Declaration of Human Rights (UDHR)**: The UDHR, adopted by the United Nations General Assembly in 1948, provided a global framework for human rights. It heavily influenced the fundamental rights provisions in the Indian Constitution, reflecting principles of equality, freedom, and human dignity.

**Constitution of United States**: The Indian Constitution's fundamental rights provisions also drew inspiration from the Constitution of the United States, particularly the Bill of Rights. Concepts such as the right to equality, freedom of speech and expression, and the right against self-incrimination have been influenced by the U.S. Constitution.

**Irish Constitution**: The Constitution of Ireland (Bunreacht na hÉireann) served as a significant source of inspiration for the Indian Constitution, especially regarding the directive principles of state policy. The Irish Constitution's emphasis on social and economic justice influenced the framers of the Indian Constitution.

**British Legal System:** India's colonial history under British rule played a role in shaping its legal system. Concepts of individual rights and the rule of law, rooted in British common law and legal traditions, influenced the inclusion of fundamental rights in the Indian Constitution.

**Indian National Movement and Social Reform Movements:** The Indian independence struggle, led by Mahatma Gandhi and various social reform movements, advocated for individual rights, equality, and justice. These movements provided the indigenous context and aspirations that influenced the framing of fundamental rights in the Indian Constitution.

While borrowing ideas and principles from various sources, the Indian Constitution tailored the concept of fundamental rights to suit the specific needs and challenges faced by the diverse society of India. The framers aimed to create a comprehensive framework of rights that would protect and promote the well-being and dignity of every individual in the country.

The fundamental rights included in the Constitution of India are a set of basic rights guaranteed to all citizens of the country. These rights are enshrined in Part III (Articles 12 to 35) of the Indian Constitution. The fundamental rights recognized in the Indian Constitution:

Right to Equality (Articles 14-18):

Equality before the law (Article 14)

Prohibition of discrimination on grounds of religion, race, caste, sex, or place of birth (Article 15)

Equality of opportunity in matters of public employment (Article 16)

Abolition of untouchability (Article 17)

Abolition of titles (Article 18)

Right to Freedom (Articles 19-22):

Freedom of speech and expression (Article 19(1)(a))

Freedom to assemble peacefully and without arms (Article 19(1)(b))

Freedom to form associations or unions (Article 19(1)(c))

Freedom to move freely throughout the territory of India (Article 19(1)(d))

Freedom to reside and settle in any part of the country (Article 19(1)(e))

Freedom to practice any profession, occupation, trade, or business (Article 19(1)(g))

Protection in respect of conviction for offenses (Article 20)

Protection of life and personal liberty (Article 21)

Protection against arrest and detention in certain cases (Article 22)

Right against Exploitation (Articles 23-24):

Prohibition of traffic in human beings and forced labor (Article 23)

Prohibition of child labor (Article 24)

Right to Freedom of Religion (Articles 25-28):

Freedom of conscience and free profession, practice, and propagation of religion (Article 25)

Freedom to manage religious affairs (Article 26)

Freedom from taxation for promotion of any religion (Article 27)

Freedom from attending religious instruction or worship in certain educational institutions (Article 28)

Cultural and Educational Rights (Articles 29-30):

Protection of interests of minorities with regard to language, script, and culture (Article 29)

Right of minorities to establish and administer educational institutions (Article 30)

Right to Constitutional Remedies (Article 32):

Right to move to the Supreme Court for the enforcement of fundamental rights.

It's important to note that these fundamental rights are not absolute and are subject to certain reasonable restrictions imposed by the state in the interest of public order, morality, health, or the rights of others. These rights play a crucial role in protecting and promoting individual liberties and ensuring social justice in India.

### 3.3) Human Rights protection in Indian Constitution:

**Overview on Human Rights Protection:**

Human rights protection refers to the safeguarding and promotion of the fundamental rights and freedoms to which all individuals are inherently entitled, regardless of their nationality, ethnicity, gender, religion, or any other status. Human rights are considered universal, inalienable, and indivisible, meaning they apply to all individuals without discrimination and cannot be taken away or separated from one another.

The protection of human rights is crucial for the establishment of a just and equitable society. It ensures that individuals have the freedom to express themselves, participate in decision-making processes, and live with dignity and equality. Governments, international organizations, and civil society have a responsibility to respect, protect, and fulfill human rights, creating an environment where individuals can exercise their rights without fear of persecution or discrimination.

**There are several key elements and mechanisms involved in human rights protection:**

International Human Rights Instruments: International legal frameworks provide a foundation for human rights protection. The Universal Declaration of Human Rights (UDHR), adopted by the United Nations General Assembly in 1948, outlines a comprehensive set of human rights standards. Additionally, various conventions, treaties, and covenants, such as the International Covenant on Civil and Political Rights (ICCPR) and the International Covenant on Economic, Social and Cultural Rights (ICESCR), further elaborate on specific rights and establish obligations for states to protect and promote them.

**National Legislation and Institutions:** Governments play a crucial role in protecting human rights by enacting national laws and establishing institutions responsible for their enforcement. Constitutional guarantees, legislative frameworks, and regulatory bodies ensure the protection of human rights at the domestic level. These include national human rights commissions, ombudsman offices, and specialized courts.

**Non-Discrimination and Equality:** Human rights protection is rooted in the principles of non-discrimination and equality. States have an obligation to ensure that all individuals are treated equally before the law and are protected from discrimination based on race, ethnicity, gender, religion, disability, sexual orientation, or any other grounds. Measures such as affirmative action policies may be implemented to address historical inequalities and ensure equal opportunities for marginalized groups.

**Access to Justice:** Effective access to justice is essential for human rights protection. Individuals should have access to fair and impartial courts, legal aid services, and remedies when their rights are violated. This includes mechanisms such as judicial review, administrative tribunals, and alternative dispute resolution methods.

**Civil Society and Advocacy:** Civil society organizations, including human rights groups, activists, and NGOs, play a vital role in advocating for human rights protection. They monitor human rights situations, raise awareness, and engage in lobbying and advocacy efforts to influence policy and promote accountability. Freedom of association, assembly, and expression are critical in enabling civil society's participation in human rights protection.

**International Human Rights Monitoring:** International and regional mechanisms are in place to monitor and ensure compliance with human rights standards. These include treaty bodies, such as the Human Rights Council and the Committee on the Elimination of Racial Discrimination, as well as regional courts and commissions, such as the European Court of Human Rights and the Inter-American Commission on Human Rights. These bodies review state reports, conduct investigations, and issue recommendation to hold states accountable for human rights violations.

**Corporate Social Responsibility**: In recent years, there has been a growing recognition of the responsibility of businesses to respect human rights. The United Nations Guiding Principles on Business and Human Rights outline the responsibilities of corporations to avoid infringing upon human rights and to address any adverse impacts resulting from their activities. This includes respecting labor rights, ensuring environmental sustainability, and preventing human rights abuses throughout their supply chains.

**Humanitarian and Refugee Protections**: Human rights protection extends to vulnerable populations, including refugees, internally displaced persons, and victims of armed conflict or natural disasters.

The Indian Constitution provides for the protection of human rights through various provisions and fundamental rights. Here are some key aspects of human rights protection in the Indian Constitution:

1. Fundamental Rights: Part III of the Indian Constitution contains fundamental rights that guarantee certain basic rights to all citizens. These rights include the right to equality, right to freedom of speech and expression, right to life and personal liberty, right to protection from discrimination, right to freedom of religion, and right to constitutional remedies.
2. Right to Equality: Article 14 of the Indian Constitution ensures equality before the law and prohibits discrimination on grounds of religion, race, caste, sex, or place of birth. It ensures that every individual is treated equally under the law.
3. Right to Freedom: Articles 19 to 22 guarantee the right to freedom of speech and expression, right to assemble peaceably and without arms, right to form associations or unions, right to move freely throughout the country, and right to reside and settle in any part of India.
4. Right to Life and Personal Liberty: Article 21 protects the right to life and personal liberty, stating that no person shall be deprived of his or her life or personal liberty except according to the procedure established by law. This provision ensures the protection of individual freedoms and safeguards against arbitrary actions by the state.

5. Right against Exploitation: Articles 23 and 24 prohibit trafficking in human beings, forced labor, and child labor. They provide for the protection of vulnerable sections of society and aim to prevent exploitation.
6. Right to Education: Article 21A was added through a constitutional amendment to provide free and compulsory education to children aged 6 to 14 years. This right ensures access to education for all children.
7. Right to Constitutional Remedies: Article 32 provides for the right to move the Supreme Court for the enforcement of fundamental rights. It empowers individuals to seek judicial remedies in case of violation of their rights.
8. Directive Principles of State Policy: Part IV of the Indian Constitution contains Directive Principles of State Policy, which are guidelines for the government to promote social justice, welfare, and protection of human rights. Though not enforceable in courts, they serve as a moral compass for the government.
9. Independent Judiciary: The Indian Constitution establishes an independent judiciary as one of the pillars of democracy. The judiciary acts as a protector of human rights by interpreting and upholding the constitutional provisions.
10. Other Laws: Apart from the constitutional provisions, various laws have been enacted to protect human rights in India, such as the Protection of Human Rights Act, 1993, which provides for the establishment of the National Human Rights Commission and State Human Rights Commissions to address human rights violations. It is important to note that while the Indian Constitution provides a robust framework for human rights protection, there are challenges in its implementation and instances of human rights violations still occur. The government and civil society continue to work towards strengthening human rights protection and addressing these challenges.

# IV
# Teaching Methods & Activities

Teaching methods and activities vary widely, each designed to engage students in meaningful learning experiences. Teaching peace education requires a blend of methods and activities that foster empathy, respect, and conflict resolution. Through lecture-based teaching, educators introduce core concepts like non-violence, tolerance, and empathy, using stories, case studies, and visual aids to bring these ideas to life and encourage students to reflect. Discussion-based methods, such as think-pair-share or group debates, enable students to explore diverse perspectives and practice respectful communication, creating a foundation of mutual understanding. Project-Based Learning (PBL) deepens students' connection to peace topics, as they work on community-centered projects like organizing peace campaigns, conducting interviews with local leaders, or creating awareness programs. Cooperative learning activities, such as the jigsaw technique, foster teamwork and responsibility, where students learn about various aspects of peace-building and then teach each other, reinforcing collective learning and accountability.

## 4.1) Methods & activities of Teaching Human Rights :

The concept of human rights refers to the fundamental rights and freedoms to which all individuals are inherently entitled, regardless of their nationality, ethnicity, gender, religion, or any other characteristic. Human rights are based on the principles of human dignity, equality, and fairness, and they are considered to be universal, inalienable, and indivisible.

Human rights encompass a wide range of civil, political, economic, social, and cultural rights. Some key examples of human rights include the right to life, liberty, and security of person; the right to freedom of thought, conscience, religion, speech, and expression; the right to a fair trial; the right to education, work, and social security; and the right to participate in cultural, artistic, and scientific life.

The concept of human rights is rooted in various historical documents and international treaties, including the Universal Declaration of Human Rights *(UDHR)* adopted by the United Nations General Assembly in 1948. The UDHR serves as a cornerstone document that sets out a comprehensive list of rights and has been instrumental in shaping subsequent human rights treaties and conventions.

Human rights are crucial for promoting and protecting the inherent dignity and worth of every individual. They provide a framework for ensuring equality, justice, and respect for all people, regardless of their background or circumstances. Human rights also establish obligations on governments and institutions to create an environment where individuals can fully enjoy their rights and hold accountable those who violate them.

While the concept of human rights is widely recognized and accepted, the realization of human rights is an ongoing challenge. Issues such as discrimination, poverty, gender inequality, armed conflicts, and authoritarian regimes continue to pose significant obstacles to the full enjoyment of human rights worldwide. Efforts to promote and protect human rights involve advocacy, education, legal frameworks, and international cooperation to address these challenges and create a more just and inclusive society.

*Teaching human rights* is a crucial aspect of fostering awareness, empathy, and respect for the rights and dignity of every individual. There are several effective methods and approaches to teach human rights. Some commonly used methods:

1. **Discussion and Debate:** Engage students in open discussions and debates on various human rights topics. Encourage them to express their opinions, analyze different perspectives, and develop critical thinking skills.

Discussion and debate are valuable methods for teaching human rights as they promote critical thinking, active participation, and the development of persuasive argumentation skills. Here are some tips for implementing discussion and debate in human rights education:

*Topic Selection:* Choose topics that are relevant, thought-provoking, and encompass a range of human rights issues. Examples include freedom of speech, gender equality, racial discrimination, LGBTQ+ rights, refugee rights, and the right to education. Consider the age and maturity of the students and select topics accordingly.

*Establish Ground Rules:* Set clear guidelines for respectful and constructive discussions. Emphasize the importance of listening to others, valuing diverse perspectives, and maintaining a safe and inclusive environment. Encourage students to challenge ideas but not individuals.

*Research and Preparation:* Before the discussion or debate, provide students with relevant background information and resources to explore the topic. Encourage them to conduct research, gather evidence, and form informed opinions. This will help them develop strong arguments and engage in meaningful dialogue.

*Structured Discussions:* Use structured discussion formats to ensure everyone has an opportunity to participate. This can include fishbowl discussions (where a smaller group discusses while others observe), Socratic seminars (where students ask questions and engage in dialogue), or small group discussions followed by a whole-class debriefing.

*Moderator or Facilitator:* Designate a student or teacher as a moderator or facilitator to guide the discussion, ensure everyone gets a chance to speak, and maintain a respectful atmosphere. The moderator can ask probing questions, encourage deeper analysis, and ensure the discussion remains focused.

*Role of Evidence:* Teach students the importance of using evidence to support their arguments. Encourage them to cite relevant laws, international human rights instruments, court cases, research studies, personal testimonies, or historical examples to strengthen their viewpoints.

*Devil's Advocate:* Assign some students the task of presenting arguments contrary to their personal beliefs. This exercise helps develop empathy, critical thinking, and the ability to understand multiple perspectives.

*Reflection and Summarization:* After the discussion or debate, provide time for students to reflect on the experience. Ask them to summarize the main arguments presented, identify areas of agreement or disagreement, and reflect on how their views may have evolved or solidified.

*Follow-Up Activities:* Extend the discussion beyond the classroom by assigning related activities. These could include writing reflections, creating persuasive essays or presentations, or conducting further research on the topic.

Remember to create a supportive and inclusive environment where all students feel comfortable expressing their opinions. Encourage respectful listening, discourage personal attacks, and foster an atmosphere that values diversity of thought.

2. **Case Studies**: Use real-life case studies to explore human rights violations or achievements. Students can examine specific situations, understand the impact on individuals or communities, and discuss possible solutions.Case studies are an effective method for teaching human rights as they provide concrete examples of real-life situations, allowing students to analyze and understand the complexities of human rights issues. Here's how you can utilize case studies in human rights education:

*Select Relevant Cases:* Choose case studies that are relevant to the human rights topics you wish to address. Select cases that are diverse in terms of geography, historical context, and human rights violations or achievements. The cases can cover a wide range of issues such as freedom of expression, torture, discrimination, right to privacy, access to education, and more.

*Provide Background Information:* Begin by providing students with essential background information about the case, including relevant historical, social, and cultural contexts. Explain the human rights principles or instruments that apply to the situation. Help students understand the significance and implications of the case.

*Analyze the Case:* Break down the case study into key components, such as the individuals or communities involved, the human rights violations or challenges they face, the relevant laws or international human rights standards, and the responses or actions taken by various stakeholders. Encourage students to identify the underlying causes and consequences of the situation.

*Promote Critical Thinking:* Engage students in critical analysis by asking probing questions. Encourage them to consider the perspectives of different actors, evaluate the ethical dilemmas involved, and explore potential solutions or strategies for addressing the human rights issues at hand.

*Group Discussion:* Divide students into small groups and assign each group a case study to analyze. Provide guiding questions to stimulate discussion and encourage students to share their findings, insights, and opinions with their group members. Afterward, conduct a whole-class discussion to facilitate further exploration and exchange of ideas.

*Reflective Writing:* Assign students individual reflective writing assignments where they can analyze the case study independently and express their personal thoughts, emotions, and reactions. This encourages introspection and deepens their understanding of the human rights issues explored in the case.

*Legal Analysis:* For more advanced students or those interested in legal aspects, encourage them to analyze the case from a legal perspective. Ask them to identify relevant human rights laws, treaties, or court decisions that apply to the situation. Discuss the implications of these legal frameworks on the case and examine the challenges in implementing and enforcing human rights standards.

*Comparative Analysis:* Encourage students to compare and contrast different case studies or human rights situations. This allows them to identify common patterns, analyze different approaches to human rights challenges, and recognize the universal principles underlying human rights.

*Action-Oriented Projects:* Inspire students to take action by designing projects that address the human rights issues highlighted in the case studies. This can involve organizing awareness campaigns, creating advocacy materials, fundraising for relevant organizations, or engaging in community service initiatives.

By using case studies, students can develop a deeper understanding of the complexities of human rights, empathy for those affected, and the motivation to work towards positive change in their communities and beyond.

3. **Role-Playing:** Assign students different roles in scenarios related to human rights. This activity helps them understand different perspectives, empathize with others, and explore the complexities of human rights issues.Role-playing is an interactive and immersive teaching method that allows students to explore human rights issues by assuming different roles and perspectives. It helps students develop empathy, critical thinking, and problem-solving skills. Here's how you can incorporate role-playing in human rights education:

*Select Appropriate Scenarios:* Choose scenarios or situations that reflect real-life human rights challenges. These can be based on historical events, current issues, or hypothetical situations. Ensure that the scenarios are relevant to the age and maturity level of your students.

*Assign Roles:* Assign students different roles, such as victims, human rights activists, government officials, journalists, community members, or representatives from international organizations. Each role should have a unique perspective and responsibilities related to the human rights issue being explored.

*Provide Background Information:* Give students the necessary background information about the scenario, including the social, cultural, and political context. Explain the human rights principles or standards relevant to the situation. Provide any relevant historical or legal information that will help students understand the nuances of the scenario.

*Set the Stage:* Create a conducive environment for role-playing. Set up the physical space accordingly, provide any necessary props or visual aids, and establish the rules and expectations for the activity. Encourage students to fully embody their roles and stay in character throughout the exercise.

*Conduct the Role-Play:* Allow students to engage in the role-play activity. Encourage them to think and respond as their assigned roles would, considering the perspectives, motivations, and challenges faced by the characters. Let them interact with one another, engage in dialogue, and negotiate possible solutions or actions.

*Debrief and Reflect:* After the role-play, facilitate a debriefing session where students can share their experiences, thoughts, and emotions. Encourage them to reflect on the impact of the scenario on their understanding of human rights issues. Discuss the challenges faced by different roles and explore the implications of their decisions or actions.

*Analyze and Evaluate:* Engage students in critical analysis of the role-play exercise. Ask questions about the ethical dilemmas encountered, the effectiveness of different approaches, and the impact on individuals or communities. Encourage students to consider the broader implications for human rights and social justice.

*Variation and Adaptation:* Experiment with different variations of role-playing, such as switching roles or introducing unexpected events during the exercise. Adapt the activity to suit the specific human rights issues or learning objectives you want to address. Allow flexibility for improvisation and creative problem-solving.

*Apply Real-Life Context:* Connect the role-play experience to real-life contexts. Help students make connections between the scenarios and actual human rights challenges faced by individuals or communities around the world. Encourage them to think about how they can translate their learning into action.

*Follow-Up Activities:* Provide opportunities for students to further explore the human rights issues addressed in the role-play through follow-up activities. This can include individual or group research, reflective writing, presentations, or creative projects that delve deeper into the topic.

Role-playing enables students to gain a deeper understanding of human rights issues by immersing themselves in the experiences and perspectives of different stakeholders. It encourages empathy, critical thinking, and the development of effective communication and negotiation skills.

4. **Multimedia and Visuals:** Utilize multimedia resources, such as documentaries, films, photographs, and news articles, to illustrate human rights concepts and current events. Visuals can enhance understanding and emotional connection to the subject matter. Utilizing multimedia and visuals is an effective method for teaching human rights as it engages students visually and emotionally, making the concepts more relatable and memorable. Here's how you can incorporate multimedia and visuals in human rights education:

*Documentaries and Films:* Show relevant documentaries or films that highlight human rights issues. Choose high-quality productions that provide in-depth exploration of the topic, present diverse perspectives, and evoke emotional responses. Follow up with discussions and reflections on the issues raised in the documentary.

*Photographs and Images:* Display powerful photographs or images that depict human rights violations, activism, or positive examples of human rights achievements. Analyze the visual elements, emotions conveyed, and the stories behind the images. Encourage students to reflect on the human rights principles and values portrayed.

*News Articles and Reports:* Share news articles, reports, or opinion pieces that cover human rights topics. Discuss current events related to human rights violations, social movements, or legal developments. Analyze the media's role in raising awareness, advocacy, or influencing public opinion on human rights issues.

*Infographics and Data Visualization:* Use infographics or data visualization tools to present statistics, trends, or comparative data related to human rights. Visual representations can help students comprehend complex information more easily and facilitate discussions on the significance and implications of the data.

*Virtual Reality (VR) and Augmented Reality (AR):* Explore the possibilities of immersive technologies like virtual reality and augmented reality. VR experiences can simulate real-life human rights situations, transporting students to different environments and allowing them to interact with the scenario. AR can overlay information or virtual objects onto the real world, enhancing understanding and engagement.

*Artistic Expression and Creative Projects:* Encourage students to create their own visual artworks, such as drawings, paintings, collages, or digital media, to express their understanding of human rights issues. Artistic expression can help students connect emotionally with the subject matter and communicate their perspectives effectively.

*Human Rights Campaigns and Advertisements:* Show examples of human rights campaigns, public service announcements, or advertisements that aim to raise awareness or advocate for human rights. Analyze the messaging, visual techniques, and strategies employed to convey a powerful and persuasive message.

*Online Multimedia Resources:* Take advantage of online platforms and resources dedicated to human rights education. Websites, interactive modules, and video platforms can provide a wealth of multimedia content, including interviews, speeches, testimonies, and educational materials on various human rights topics.

*Guest Speakers and Expert Panels:* Invite human rights activists, experts, or individuals with lived experiences to share their stories and insights using multimedia elements such as videos, photos, or personal narratives. This brings real-world perspectives and firsthand accounts into the classroom, fostering empathy and understanding.

*Multimedia Presentations and Projects:* Assign students multimedia projects where they create presentations, videos, or digital stories on human rights topics. This allows them to research, analyze, and present their findings creatively, utilizing multimedia elements to enhance their message.

When incorporating multimedia and visuals, ensure that you provide context, facilitate discussions, and encourage critical analysis of the content. The visual and emotional impact of multimedia resources can effectively engage students, deepen their understanding, and foster a sense of empathy and responsibility towards human rights issues.

5. **Community Engagement:** Encourage students to participate in community service projects or initiatives related to human rights. This hands-on approach allows them to witness human rights issues firsthand and develop a sense of social responsibility. Community engagement is a powerful method for teaching human rights that allows students to connect

with real-world issues, develop empathy, and actively contribute to positive change. Here are some ways to incorporate community engagement in human rights education:

*Service-Learning Projects:* Design service-learning projects that address human rights issues in the local community. This can involve partnering with local organizations, conducting research, organizing awareness campaigns, or engaging in direct service activities that promote human rights.

*Volunteer Opportunities:* Identify volunteer opportunities with organizations working on human rights-related causes. Encourage students to get involved and contribute their time and skills to support initiatives such as providing assistance to refugees, working with marginalized communities, or promoting equality and inclusion.

*Community Events and Workshops:* Organize or participate in community events, workshops, or panel discussions focused on human rights topics. Collaborate with local organizations, activists, or community leaders to create platforms for dialogue, education, and awareness raising.

*Advocacy and Activism:* Guide students in developing their advocacy skills by encouraging them to raise awareness about human rights issues. This can involve organizing protests, writing letters to policymakers, creating petitions, or using social media platforms to share information and advocate for change.

*Cultural Exchanges:* Facilitate cultural exchanges or dialogues that promote understanding, respect, and appreciation for diverse cultures and identities. Partner with local schools or organizations to create opportunities for students to interact with individuals from different backgrounds and learn about their experiences and perspectives.

*Guest Speakers and Field Visits:* Invite guest speakers from human rights organizations, local community leaders, or individuals who have experienced human rights violations. Arrange field visits to relevant institutions or organizations, such as a local court, a human rights commission, or a refugee center, to provide students with firsthand experiences and insights.

*Collaborative Projects:* Encourage students to collaborate on projects with community organizations or individuals. This can involve creating educational resources, conducting research, or developing initiatives that address specific human rights issues identified by the community.

*Human Rights Awareness Campaigns:* Engage students in designing and implementing human rights awareness campaigns in their schools or communities. This can include organizing workshops, creating educational materials, or hosting events to promote understanding, tolerance, and respect for human rights.

*Partnerships with Local Organizations:* Foster partnerships with local human rights organizations, nonprofits, or community centers. Collaborate with these organizations to provide resources, expertise, and guidance for students' engagement in human rights activities.

*Reflection and Action Plans:* Ensure that community engagement activities are followed by reflection and action planning. Encourage students to reflect on their experiences, assess the impact of their actions, and develop strategies for continued engagement in human rights issues.

Community engagement allows students to see the relevance of human rights in their own communities and empowers them to take action. It provides valuable opportunities for experiential learning, promoting empathy, critical thinking, and a sense of social responsibility in students.

**Other methods of Teaching Human Rights include:**

Simulations and Games: Use interactive simulations or educational games that simulate human rights challenges. These activities engage students actively, encouraging problem-solving, decision-making, and understanding of the complexities involved.

Artistic Expression: Encourage students to express their understanding of human rights through art, music, creative writing, or drama. This allows for personal reflection and exploration of emotions related to human rights.

Comparative Studies: Compare human rights systems and practices across different countries or cultures. This approach helps students recognize cultural differences, appreciate diverse perspectives, and understand the universality of human rights.

Research and Projects: Assign research projects on human rights topics, requiring students to delve into historical events, legal frameworks, or contemporary issues. This promotes independent thinking, information gathering, and analytical skills.

It's important to adapt teaching methods to the age, maturity level, and cultural context of the students. Creating a safe and inclusive learning environment is essential for effective human rights education.

4.2) **Obstacles of Human Rights Education:**

Human rights education is a process that aims to promote awareness, understanding, and respect for human rights among individuals and communities. It involves teaching and learning about human rights principles, values, and standards, as well as the skills necessary to promote and protect human rights in everyday life. Human rights education encompasses both formal and informal education settings, including schools, universities, community organizations, and various media platforms.

The goals of human rights education are manifold. They include:

1. Promoting awareness: Human rights education seeks to increase awareness about human rights, ensuring that individuals understand their fundamental rights and the rights of others. It aims to foster a sense of empathy and responsibility toward all members of society.
2. Developing knowledge and understanding: Human rights education provides knowledge about the international and regional human rights frameworks, including the Universal Declaration of Human Rights and other relevant treaties and instruments. It also explores the historical, cultural, and social contexts that shape human rights issues.
3. Nurturing attitudes and values: Human rights education aims to cultivate attitudes of respect, tolerance, equality, and non-discrimination. It seeks to challenge prejudice, stereotypes, and discriminatory practices, promoting a culture of human rights and social justice.
4. Building skills: Human rights education equips individuals with the skills needed to address human rights issues effectively. These skills include critical thinking, dialogue and negotiation, advocacy, conflict resolution, and active citizenship. Human rights education empowers individuals to take action to protect and promote human rights in their communities and beyond.
5. Fostering a culture of human rights: Human rights education aims to create a culture that respects and upholds human rights. By integrating human rights principles into various aspects of society, such as education, law, governance, and media, it seeks to transform attitudes, behaviors, and structures to ensure the realization of human rights for all. Human rights education can take various forms, such as formal classroom teaching, extracurricular activities, workshops, seminars, online courses, and awareness campaigns. It can be tailored to different

age groups, cultural contexts, and specific human rights issues. Overall, human rights education plays a crucial role in promoting social justice, equality, and dignity for all individuals, and in preventing human rights abuses.

Human rights education is crucial for promoting awareness, understanding, and respect for human rights principles and values. However, there are several obstacles that can impede the effective implementation of human rights education:

- Lack of awareness and understanding: Many people may not be aware of their rights or have a limited understanding of human rights concepts. This lack of awareness can hinder the development and implementation of human rights education programs.
- Cultural and societal barriers: Human rights values and principles may conflict with cultural or societal norms and practices in certain regions or communities. These cultural and societal barriers can create resistance or opposition to human rights education initiatives.
- Political resistance: Governments or authorities may be resistant to human rights education if it challenges their authority or exposes human rights abuses. They may limit or censor educational materials or curricula that promote critical thinking or dissenting views.
- Insufficient resources: Human rights education requires adequate resources, including funding, trained educators, and appropriate teaching materials. In many cases, there is a lack of financial and logistical support for the development and implementation of comprehensive human rights education programs.
- Limited access to education: In many parts of the world, access to quality education is limited, especially for marginalized groups, such as women, children, refugees, or individuals from low-income backgrounds. The lack of access to education itself poses a significant obstacle to human rights education.
- Prejudice and discrimination: Deep-rooted prejudice, discrimination, and biases based on race, ethnicity, religion, gender, sexual orientation, or other factors can impede the effective teaching and learning of human rights principles. Overcoming these biases is crucial for promoting inclusive and equitable human rights education.

- Lack of institutional support: Educational institutions, including schools and universities, may not prioritize human rights education or provide sufficient support for integrating it into their curricula. The absence of institutional support can hinder the sustainability and impact of human rights education initiatives.
- Language and cultural barriers: Human rights education materials and resources may not be available or accessible in local languages or may not be culturally relevant. Language and cultural barriers can limit the effectiveness of human rights education in reaching diverse populations.

Addressing these obstacles requires a multi-faceted approach involving governments, civil society organizations, educators, and communities. It involves raising awareness, promoting inclusive policies, providing adequate resources, training educators, and fostering an environment that values and respects human rights.

**4.3) National Human Rights Commission (NHRC):**

The National Human Rights Commission (NHRC) of India was established in 1993 to protect and promote human rights in the country. The creation of the NHRC was a significant milestone in India's human rights journey. Here is a brief history of the NHRC in India:

Background:

The need for an independent human rights institution in India was recognized during the 1990s when there were growing concerns about human rights violations. India had already ratified various international human rights treaties, including the International Covenant on Civil and Political Rights and the Convention Against Torture, and needed a national mechanism to fulfill its obligations.

The Protection of Human Rights Act, 1993:

The Protection of Human Rights Act, 1993 was enacted by the Parliament of India, which provided the legal framework for the establishment of the NHRC. The Act defined the composition, functions, and powers of the NHRC, ensuring its independence and effectiveness.

Establishment of the NHRC:

The NHRC was formally constituted on October 12, 1993, with retired Chief Justice of India, Shri Ranganath Misra, as its first Chairperson. The NHRC consists of a Chairperson and members appointed by the President of India. The Chairperson should be a retired Chief Justice of India, and the members should include judges of the Supreme Court, High Court, and eminent persons from various fields.

Mandate and Functions:

The NHRC is mandated to investigate and inquire into allegations of human rights violations, either suo motu (on its own) or based on complaints received. It has the power to visit prisons, detention centers, and other places of custody to ensure the protection of human rights. The NHRC can also recommend compensation to victims and take measures for their rehabilitation.

Expansion of Powers:

Over the years, the NHRC's powers have been expanded through amendments to the Protection of Human Rights Act. These amendments have provided the NHRC with additional investigative and administrative powers, such as the power to recommend prosecution and the authority to inquire into matters concerning the armed forces.

**Impact and Role:**

The NHRC has played a significant role in addressing human rights issues in India. It has intervened in cases of custodial deaths, police excesses, bonded labor, violations of the rights of marginalized communities, and more. The NHRC's recommendations and reports have influenced policy and legal reforms, leading to improvements in the human rights situation in the country.

Regional and International Engagement:

The NHRC actively engages with regional and international human rights institutions. It collaborates with other national human rights institutions, participates in meetings of the Asia Pacific Forum of National Human Rights Institutions, and engages with the United Nations human rights mechanisms.

The National Human Rights Commission of India continues to work towards the protection and promotion of human rights, addressing violations, raising awareness, and advocating for necessary reforms.

The National Human Rights Commission (NHRC) is a government body that is responsible for the protection and promotion of human rights within a particular country. While the specifics of each country's NHRC may vary, I can provide you with general information about human rights commissions.

Functions and Responsibilities:

Investigation and Inquiry: NHRCs have the authority to investigate complaints or allegations of human rights violations. They can inquire into matters either on their own initiative or upon receiving a complaint from individuals or organizations.

Monitoring and Reporting: NHRCs monitor the overall human rights situation in the country, including issues related to civil, political, economic, social, and cultural rights. They publish reports and recommendations to draw attention to human rights concerns and suggest measures to address them.

Advocacy and Public Awareness: NHRCs play a crucial role in raising awareness about human rights and promoting a culture of respect for human rights. They engage in educational and outreach activities to inform the public about their rights and responsibilities.

Legal Intervention and Remedies: NHRCs may have the power to intervene in legal proceedings involving human rights violations. They can initiate legal action or intervene as a party to seek remedies for victims of human rights abuses.

Policy and Legislative Recommendations: NHRCs provide recommendations to the government on policies, legislation, and administrative measures necessary for the effective protection and promotion of human rights.

Collaboration and Cooperation: NHRCs often collaborate with other governmental and non-governmental entities, including international organizations, to strengthen human rights protection. They may participate in regional and international human rights forums to share experiences and best practices.

Independence:
An NHRC is typically designed to be an independent and impartial body. It operates autonomously from the government and other authorities to ensure its objectivity in the examination of human rights issues. The independence of an NHRC is crucial for it to effectively fulfill its mandate.

International Standards:
NHRCs are often established in accordance with international human rights standards and principles. These standards, such as those outlined in the Universal Declaration of Human Rights and other international conventions, guide the work of NHRCs and help ensure that human rights are protected in a comprehensive and consistent manner.

It's important to note that the specifics of an NHRC's powers, functions, and structure may vary from country to country, as each nation has its own legal framework and system for human rights protection.

**Role:**

The National Human Rights Commission (NHRC) plays a crucial role in the protection and promotion of human rights within a country. Its primary functions and responsibilities include:

Investigation and Inquiry: The NHRC has the authority to investigate complaints or allegations of human rights violations. It can inquire into matters either on its own initiative or upon receiving complaints from individuals or organizations. This includes conducting fact-finding missions, gathering evidence, and interviewing relevant parties.

Monitoring and Reporting: The NHRC monitors the overall human rights situation in the country. It collects data, receives reports, and analyzes trends to identify systemic issues and areas of concern. The NHRC publishes reports and recommendations to draw attention to human rights concerns, inform the public, and urge the government and relevant authorities to take appropriate actions.

Advocacy and Public Awareness: The NHRC plays a vital role in raising awareness about human rights and promoting a culture of respect for human rights. It engages in educational and outreach activities to inform the public about their rights and responsibilities. This includes organizing seminars, workshops, and campaigns to disseminate information and encourage dialogue on human rights issues.

Legal Intervention and Remedies: The NHRC may have the power to intervene in legal proceedings involving human rights violations. It can initiate legal action or intervene as a party to seek remedies for victims of human rights abuses. The NHRC can recommend compensation, restitution, or other forms of relief for individuals or communities affected by human rights violations.

Policy and Legislative Recommendations: The NHRC provides recommendations to the government on policies, legislation, and administrative measures necessary for the effective protection and promotion of human rights. It advises on human rights standards, advocates for legal reforms, and suggests changes to existing laws or practices that may infringe upon human rights.

Collaboration and Cooperation: The NHRC collaborates with other governmental and non-governmental entities to strengthen human rights protection. It may work with law enforcement agencies, civil society organizations, and international institutions to share information, coordinate efforts, and promote human rights at various levels. The NHRC also participates in regional and international human rights forums to exchange experiences and best practices.

Public Complaints Redressal: The NHRC provides a platform for individuals to file complaints regarding human rights violations. It receives, registers, and addresses complaints, ensuring that victims have a mechanism to seek redressal for the violation of their rights. The NHRC facilitates mediation, conciliation, and other dispute resolution processes to resolve complaints and provide justice to affected individuals.

Overall, the NHRC acts as a watchdog, protector, and advocate for human rights, working towards ensuring that human rights are respected, protected, and fulfilled for all individuals within its jurisdiction.

**4.3.2) State Human Rights Commission (SHRC):**

The establishment of State Human Rights Commissions (SHRCs) in India can be traced back to the enactment of the Protection of Human Rights Act, 1993. This act was passed by the Parliament of India to give effect to the provisions of the Universal Declaration of Human Rights and other international human rights instruments.

Prior to the enactment of this act, the National Human Rights Commission (NHRC) was established at the national level in 1993 to protect and promote human rights in India. Recognizing the need for a similar mechanism at the state level, the Protection of Human Rights Act, 1993, provided for the establishment of SHRCs in each state.

The historical background of SHRCs in India is rooted in the broader context of the human rights movement and the recognition of the importance of safeguarding and promoting human rights. The establishment of these commissions was a significant step towards ensuring the protection of human rights at the state level and bringing justice to the victims of human rights violations.

The Protection of Human Rights Act, 1993, set out the framework for the establishment, composition, powers, and functions of SHRCs. It defined the mandate of the commissions, their jurisdiction, and the procedures for filing complaints and conducting inquiries.

Since the enactment of the Protection of Human Rights Act, SHRCs have been established in various states across India. These commissions have played a crucial role in investigating complaints of human rights violations, recommending appropriate actions, and ensuring justice for the victims. They have also contributed to raising awareness about human rights and promoting a culture of respect for human rights in their respective states.

Over the years, SHRCs have faced challenges and limitations in terms of their independence, effectiveness, and capacity. Efforts have been made to strengthen these commissions and enhance their effectiveness in addressing human rights issues. The functioning of SHRCs is subject to periodic review and reforms to ensure their alignment with international human rights standards and best practices.

Overall, the establishment of State Human Rights Commissions in India has been a significant development in the country's human rights landscape, providing a dedicated mechanism for the protection and promotion of human rights at the state level.

A State Human Rights Commission (SHRC) is a statutory body established at the state level in India to protect and promote human rights. These commissions are independent organizations that investigate complaints of human rights violations and take appropriate action to ensure justice and redress for the victims.

Each state in India has its own State Human Rights Commission, established under the Protection of Human Rights Act, 1993. The composition, powers, and functions of these commissions may vary slightly from state to state, but they generally have the following responsibilities:

Inquiry and investigation: SHRCs have the authority to inquire into complaints of human rights violations, either suo motu (on their own initiative) or based on complaints received from individuals or groups.

Recommendation and intervention: These commissions can recommend appropriate actions, remedies, and interventions to the concerned authorities, such as government departments, law enforcement agencies, or the judiciary, to ensure justice for the victims and prevent further violations.

Public awareness and education: SHRCs play a crucial role in creating awareness about human rights, conducting educational programs, and promoting a culture of respect for human rights among the general public.

Legal assistance and support: These commissions can provide legal aid and support to victims of human rights violations, including access to legal representation and counseling services.

Monitoring and review: SHRCs monitor the implementation of human rights safeguards, policies, and laws by the state government and other authorities. They also review existing laws and suggest necessary reforms to align with international human rights standards.

It's important to note that the specific details and functioning of State Human Rights Commissions may vary from state to state.

**Role:**

The State Human Rights Commissions (SHRCs) in India play a crucial role in the protection and promotion of human rights at the state level. Here are some of the key roles and functions of SHRCs:

Inquiry and investigation: SHRCs have the authority to inquire into complaints of human rights violations within their respective states. They can initiate investigations either suo motu (on their own accord) or based on complaints filed by individuals or groups. The commissions have the power to summon witnesses, examine evidence, and take appropriate action in response to human rights violations.

Recommendation and intervention: SHRCs can recommend appropriate actions, remedies, and interventions to the concerned authorities, such as government departments, law enforcement agencies, or the judiciary. These recommendations aim to ensure justice for the victims, provide compensation or rehabilitation, and prevent further violations.

Public awareness and education: SHRCs have a responsibility to raise awareness about human rights among the general public. They conduct awareness campaigns, educational programs, and workshops to promote a culture of respect for human rights and to disseminate information about the rights and entitlements of individuals.

Legal assistance and support: SHRCs can provide legal aid and support to victims of human rights violations. This may include facilitating access to legal representation, counseling services, and other forms of assistance to ensure the protection and realization of human rights.

Monitoring and review: SHRCs monitor the implementation of human rights safeguards, policies, and laws by the state government and other authorities. They assess the compliance of state agencies with human rights standards and recommend necessary reforms or improvements to align with international human rights obligations.

Research and studies: SHRCs undertake research, studies, and documentation of human rights issues and trends within their states. This helps in identifying systemic issues, addressing emerging challenges, and formulating policies and strategies for the effective protection and promotion of human rights.

Collaboration and coordination: SHRCs collaborate with various stakeholders, including government bodies, non-governmental organizations, and civil society groups, to address human rights issues. They engage in dialogue and coordination with these entities to promote a holistic approach to human rights protection and to address systemic human rights challenges.

It's important to note that the specific roles and functions of SHRCs may vary from state to state, as the composition, powers, and procedures of these commissions are governed by the respective state legislations and regulations.

# V

# Adult Education and Distance Education

## 5.1 Concept of Adult Education

Adult Education refers to the practice of providing learning opportunities for adults beyond traditional schooling age. It encompasses a wide range of programs and activities designed to meet the diverse needs and interests of adult learners, including continuing education, workforce training, personal enrichment, and literacy programs. Adult education aims to empower individuals by enhancing their skills, knowledge, and competencies, thereby enabling them to achieve their personal, professional, and societal goals. It often takes place in various settings, such as community centers, colleges, workplaces, and online platforms, and may be formal or informal in nature.

Adult education encompasses a broad spectrum of learning opportunities tailored to individuals beyond traditional schooling age. Its primary focus is on meeting the diverse needs and interests of adult learners, fostering personal growth, skill development, and lifelong learning. This field recognizes that education is not confined to childhood or adolescence and that adults continually seek opportunities to acquire new knowledge, skills, and competencies throughout their lives.

The concept of adult education acknowledges the unique characteristics and circumstances of adult learners, including their varied backgrounds, experiences, motivations, and responsibilities. Unlike traditional education, which often follows a structured curriculum and timetable, adult education programs are flexible and learner-centered, allowing individuals to pursue learning at their own pace and according to their specific interests and goals.

*Definitions* of adult education vary depending on the context and perspective of the stakeholders involved. Some common definitions include:

- ***The UNESCO Definition***: The United Nations Educational, Scientific and Cultural Organization (UNESCO) defines adult education as "the entire body of organized educational processes, whatever the content, level and method, whether formal or informal, whereby persons regarded as adults by the society to which they belong, develop their abilities, enrich their knowledge, improve their technical or professional qualifications or turn them in a new direction and bring about changes in their attitudes or behavior in the twofold perspective of full personal development and participation in balanced and independent social, economic and cultural development."
- ***Malcolm Knowles' Andragogy***: Malcolm Knowles, a pioneer in adult education, defined it as "the process of engaging adult learners in the acquisition of knowledge, skills, attitudes, and values."
- ***Lifelong Learning Perspective:*** From a lifelong learning perspective, adult education encompasses all learning activities undertaken throughout one's life, including formal education, informal learning experiences, and self-directed study aimed at personal and professional development.
- ***Functional Literacy Approach:*** In the context of literacy programs, adult education may be defined as the provision of basic literacy and numeracy skills to individuals who lack them, enabling them to participate more fully in society and improve their quality of life.
- "All the learning activities that occur after an individual has completed his basic education" -***Cooper***
- ***In the words of Darkenwald & Merriam (1982)*** "*Adult Education is a process whereby persons whose major social roles are characteristic of adult status undertake systematic and sustained learning activities for the purpose of bringing about changes in knowledge, attitude values or skills*".

Adult education is a dynamic field that addresses the diverse learning needs of adults, promotes lifelong learning, and contributes to individual empowerment, social inclusion, and economic development.

### 5.1.1 Need of Adult Education: A Comprehensive Perspective

Adult education is pivotal for fostering personal growth, societal advancement & economic development. Its significance extends beyond basic literacy ,offering adults a second chance at education and empowering them in various aspects of life. dult education plays a crucial role in empowering individuals and communities. It is not merely about literacy but encompasses a wide range of learning opportunities for adults to acquire new knowledge, skills, and competencies. As the world changes rapidly due to technological advancements, evolving job markets, and shifting social dynamics, adult education becomes increasingly important for personal, social, and economic growth. Here's an in-depth look at its significance:

*1. Promotes Lifelong Learning:* In today's fast-paced world, education cannot be limited to formal schooling in childhood or adolescence. Lifelong learning is vital to adapting to the continuous flow of new information, technology, and societal changes. Adult education nurtures this spirit of learning by offering opportunities for individuals to keep their knowledge and skills up-to-date throughout their lives. Whether it's learning new software, mastering a language, or acquiring problem-solving skills, adults need to stay competitive and informed.

*2. Enhances Employment Opportunities:* The job market today is more dynamic than ever, with industries constantly evolving. For many adults, acquiring additional education can mean the difference between stagnation and progress in their careers. Through adult education programs, individuals can upskill or reskill, making them more attractive to employers. In cases of career shifts due to automation or technological disruptions, adult education becomes a lifeline, providing new career paths and opportunities.

*3. Reduces Illiteracy and Education Gaps:* In many parts of the world, adult education addresses gaps left by traditional education systems. Millions of adults lack basic literacy and numeracy skills, hindering their ability to participate fully in society and the economy. Adult education programs targeting literacy and vocational training help adults catch up on missed education and improve their quality of life. This, in turn, breaks the cycle of poverty and opens doors to better opportunities for their families and communities.

*4. Empowers Individuals and Boosts Confidence:* Education is empowering. Adults who take part in educational programs gain self-confidence, independence, and a sense of purpose. Whether it's learning new skills to enhance employment or taking up hobbies and interests, education can boost self-esteem and mental well-being. It equips individuals with the knowledge to make informed decisions about health, finances, and family, and fosters a greater sense of autonomy in their personal lives.

5. *Reduces Social Inequality:* Education is a powerful tool in addressing inequality. Adult education programs provide access to learning for marginalized or disadvantaged groups, such as women, ethnic minorities, and people from low-income backgrounds. By offering flexible learning options, including part-time and online courses, adult education helps people who may not have had access to formal education earlier in life. These programs create pathways to better-paying jobs, thereby reducing social and economic inequality.

6. *Fosters Civic Engagement and Social Responsibility:* An educated population is more likely to engage in civic activities such as voting, community service, and advocacy for social change. Adult education can raise awareness about political, social, and environmental issues, empowering citizens to participate actively in their communities and make a positive difference. Informed adults can also become leaders in their communities, driving initiatives that promote collective well-being.

7. *Improves Quality of Life:* Adult education has a profound impact on overall life satisfaction. Learning new skills can increase financial stability and job security, which, in turn, improves mental health and reduces stress. Moreover, education improves people's ability to understand health information, make better dietary choices, and adopt healthier lifestyles. All of these contribute to a higher quality of life, not just for the individual but also for their families.

8. *Supports Economic Growth and National Development:* A well-educated adult population is essential for a country's economic development. Educated workers are more productive, innovative, and adaptable to new technologies and business practices. By creating a more skilled workforce, adult education boosts a country's competitive advantage in the global economy. Governments and businesses also benefit from adult education as it leads to higher economic participation rates and reduces unemployment.

9. *Adapting to Technological Changes:* In the era of the Fourth Industrial Revolution, technology is rapidly transforming every sector. Many adults may not have received formal education in digital skills, which are increasingly essential in today's workplaces. Adult education programs provide courses on digital literacy, enabling people to navigate new

technologies, from basic computer skills to advanced software. This helps bridge the digital divide, ensuring that adults remain employable and socially engaged.

*10. Personal Fulfillment and Social Inclusion:* For many adults, the opportunity to pursue education later in life is personally fulfilling. It opens up avenues for exploring passions, whether that's through creative writing, history, art, or science. For others, adult education is a means to reintegrate into society, especially for those who may have been marginalized or excluded due to socioeconomic factors. It promotes social inclusion, fostering communities where all members feel valued and respected.

Adult education is not just a tool for personal development but a necessity for societal progress. It contributes to building resilient individuals who can cope with the complexities of modern life while ensuring that no one is left behind in the journey of knowledge acquisition. As a transformative force, adult education helps bridge the gap between past inequities and future opportunities, making it a cornerstone for sustainable and inclusive development. Governments, organizations, and educational institutions must prioritize and invest in adult education to create a better-informed, skilled, and prosperous society.

### 5.1.2 Importance of Adult Education & Life Long Learning

In the contemporary world, education is no longer limited to childhood or the early years of life. The global landscape is characterized by rapid technological advancements, economic changes, and social shifts, which require individuals to continually update their skills and knowledge throughout life. Adult education and lifelong learning thus become essential for personal development, societal progress, and economic success. This below detailed elaboration explores the importance of adult education, accompanied by real-world examples:

*i) Enhancing Employability and Career Development:* One of the primary reasons adult education is critical is its direct impact on employability. With evolving job markets and the automation of many traditional roles, many adults find themselves needing to acquire new skills to remain relevant. Adult education offers vocational and technical courses that help individuals transition into new careers, update existing skills, or obtain promotions within their current jobs. For example, as industries like manufacturing and retail embrace automation, workers may need to retrain for jobs in programming, robotics, or data analysis. Adult education programs designed to reskill or upskill individuals become crucial for job security and career advancement.

*Example:* A factory worker who has spent years on an assembly line might enroll in a technical course in robotics. After completing the course, they can work as a technician responsible for maintaining and programming robotic systems, ensuring continued employment in an automated environment.

**ii) Bridging the Education Gap:** Many adults were unable to complete their formal education due to economic, social, or family-related challenges. Adult education provides a second chance for individuals to pursue education, improving their overall life prospects. By enabling people to gain literacy, numeracy, and even higher-level qualifications, adult education helps individuals who may have been left behind during their younger years.

*Example:* A single mother who had to leave school at a young age to support her family might return to education through an evening diploma program. This opportunity allows her to pursue her high school diploma and later, a college degree, which can lead to better job opportunities and financial independence.

**iii) Empowerment and Self-Efficacy:** Education empowers individuals by giving them the knowledge and skills necessary to navigate personal and professional challenges. Adult education contributes to self-efficacy—the belief in one's ability to achieve goals—by providing adults with the confidence to take control of their lives.

*Example:* A retired individual may decide to take a course in entrepreneurship. With newly acquired business knowledge, they might launch a small business, applying what they learned about marketing, finance, and customer relations. The education not only empowers them to earn additional income but also boosts their confidence in managing and growing a venture at an older age.

**iv) Promoting Civic Participation and Social Engagement:** Educated adults are more likely to participate in democratic processes, engage in community services, and advocate for social change. Adult education fosters civic engagement by raising awareness about societal issues and teaching individuals how to take an active role in their communities.

*Example:* After attending a community-based adult education program on environmental sustainability, an adult may take the initiative to start a local recycling program or join environmental advocacy efforts. This sense of responsibility and participation is directly linked to the education they received.

***v) Improving Health and Well-being:*** Research shows that education is closely linked to better health outcomes. Adults who receive education about nutrition, fitness, mental health, and preventative care are more likely to adopt healthier lifestyles. Adult education can also address specific issues like chronic disease management, leading to longer, healthier lives.

*Example:* A person living with diabetes might enroll in an adult education course focused on disease management. Through this course, they learn how to monitor their glucose levels, adjust their diet, and incorporate physical exercise into their daily routine, significantly improving their quality of life.

***vi) Fostering Social Inclusion:*** Adult education serves as a tool for promoting social inclusion, especially for marginalized communities. By offering flexible learning options (such as evening classes, online programs, or part-time studies), adult education creates opportunities for those who face barriers to traditional education. This inclusivity leads to greater social cohesion and a more equitable society.

*Example:* Immigrants often face barriers such as language proficiency and cultural differences when integrating into a new society. Adult education programs that offer language classes and cultural orientation help immigrants overcome these challenges, enabling them to participate more fully in their new communities.

### Concept of Lifelong Learning

*Lifelong learning* refers to the continuous, self-motivated pursuit of knowledge for personal or professional reasons throughout an individual's life. It emphasizes the idea that education is an ongoing process, not confined to formal schooling. Lifelong learning encompasses all learning activities, whether formal (structured programs), non-formal (workshops, online courses), or informal (learning through experience, self-study, etc.).

***a) Adapting to Technological Changes:*** Technology is evolving rapidly, and people must continually update their skills to keep pace. Lifelong learning ensures that individuals can adapt to new tools, systems, and methodologies in their personal and professional lives. Example: A marketing professional may enroll in a series of online courses on digital marketing strategies, social media advertising, and data analytics, keeping up with the latest trends in a constantly evolving field.

***b) Maintaining Cognitive Abilities:*** Lifelong learning helps individuals maintain cognitive abilities as they age. Research has shown that engaging in mentally stimulating activities, such as learning new languages, solving puzzles, or acquiring new skills, can delay cognitive decline and improve memory function. Example: An elderly person might take up learning a new language or playing a musical instrument as part of a lifelong learning initiative, keeping their mind sharp and active.

*c) Nurturing Personal Fulfillment and Creativity:* Lifelong learning allows individuals to pursue hobbies and interests that bring personal fulfillment and joy. Whether learning a new craft, exploring photography, or studying philosophy, lifelong learning enriches life by offering new perspectives and creative outlets. Example: A middle-aged individual with a lifelong passion for painting might enroll in art classes, eventually displaying their work in local exhibitions or galleries. The process of learning and mastering the craft not only brings fulfillment but also connects them to a community of like-minded individuals.

*d) Promoting Flexibility and Adaptability:* In a world where industries are disrupted and job roles are redefined, individuals who engage in lifelong learning are better equipped to handle changes. Learning new skills and exploring diverse fields enables people to be more flexible in their career paths and personal lives. Example: A software developer who primarily works in front-end development might take a series of courses in data science and machine learning. This additional knowledge allows them to shift career paths or take on more advanced roles in artificial intelligence-related projects.

*e) Fostering Intergenerational Learning:* Lifelong learning also promotes knowledge-sharing between generations. Older adults, with their years of experience, can mentor younger learners, while younger individuals can teach their older counterparts about new technologies and trends, fostering a mutually beneficial learning environment. Example: In a workplace, older employees with extensive experience might conduct workshops on leadership or industry history, while younger employees lead sessions on emerging technologies or digital marketing strategies.

Adult education and lifelong learning are indispensable in today's ever-evolving world. They provide adults with the skills, knowledge, and confidence needed to adapt to changing environments, improve their personal and professional lives, and contribute meaningfully to society. Whether it's empowering individuals to secure better jobs, helping them maintain cognitive vitality, or promoting social inclusion, the benefits of continued education throughout life are immense. Education, at any stage of life, is the key to unlocking opportunities, realizing potential, and fostering growth—for individuals and communities alike.

### 5.2.1 National Literacy Mission

***An Overview***

The National Literacy Mission (NLM) was launched by the Government of India in 1988 with the primary aim of eradicating illiteracy among adults and providing them with functional literacy skills. It represents one of the largest adult education programs globally, focusing on empowering individuals through literacy, promoting social and economic development, and encouraging democratic participation. The NLM sought to make 80 million people literate by 1995, with a focus on adults in the age group of 15 to 35 years.

*Beginning* of the National Literacy Mission India, at the time of its independence in 1947, had an alarmingly low literacy rate of just around 12%. Despite several efforts made in the post-independence era, the literacy rate remained quite low, particularly among disadvantaged groups, rural populations, and women. The government recognized that illiteracy was one of the key barriers to India's social and economic development.

In this context, the National Policy on Education (NPE) 1986 provided the framework for addressing the literacy challenge. It emphasized the need for a national mission dedicated to improving literacy rates, particularly among adults. In response to this policy, the National Literacy Mission (NLM) was launched in May 1988, with the ambitious goal of achieving full literacy by providing functional literacy to non-literate adults.

The mission came into being under the guidance of the Department of Education, Ministry of Human Resource Development, and was designed as a time-bound initiative aimed at imparting reading, writing, and arithmetic skills to adults. The mission was particularly focused on rural areas, marginalized communities, and women, who were most affected by illiteracy.

### Objectives of the National Literacy Mission

The National Literacy Mission had several key objectives:

*i) Eradicate Illiteracy:* The primary goal was to ensure that non-literate individuals, especially adults, gained the ability to read, write, and perform basic arithmetic functions.

*ii) Promote Functional Literacy:* The mission aimed not just at teaching people to read and write but to make them functionally literate. This means that learners would be able to use literacy to improve their quality of life by being able to handle day-to-day tasks such as reading labels, understanding instructions, and managing finances.

*iii) Empowerment through Education:* The mission sought to empower individuals by giving them the tools to improve their social, economic, and political participation. Literacy was seen as a means to foster self-reliance and active participation in society.

*iv) Reduce Gender Disparities:* One of the critical objectives was to reduce the literacy gap between men and women. Women were a major target group since they had significantly lower literacy rates, particularly in rural areas.

*v) Achieve Literacy in Regional Languages:* The NLM recognized India's linguistic diversity and aimed to impart literacy in the learner's mother tongue or regional language, promoting cultural preservation while fostering learning.

*vi) Encourage Community Participation:* The mission encouraged a decentralized, community-based approach to literacy by involving local institutions, panchayats, voluntary organizations, and individuals in the education process.

**Structure and Working of the National Literacy Mission**

The National Literacy Mission adopted a two-pronged strategy: (i) Total Literacy Campaigns (TLCs) and (ii) Post-Literacy Programs. These initiatives worked in tandem to make individuals literate and ensure that literacy skills were retained and applied in practical life.

*1. Total Literacy Campaign (TLC):* The TLC was the primary vehicle for achieving the NLM's goals. It focused on mass literacy, targeting entire districts or regions in a time-bound manner. These campaigns involved:

• Awareness Programs: The first step of the TLC was creating awareness about the importance of literacy. Mass mobilization through rallies, cultural programs, posters, and media campaigns helped convey the value of literacy in improving daily life.

• Volunteer-Based Teaching: The TLCs relied heavily on volunteers from the local community who served as teachers, mentors, and organizers. These volunteers would receive basic training and then work to impart literacy skills to learners.

• Conducive Learning Environment: Learning centers were set up in villages, schools, and community halls, making literacy education accessible to as many people as possible.

• Flexible Learning: Recognizing that many adult learners had limited time due to work and family responsibilities, the TLCs emphasized flexible timings for classes to suit learners' schedules.

**2. *Post-Literacy Campaigns:*** Once basic literacy was achieved through TLCs, Post-Literacy Programs were implemented to ensure that newly literate individuals retained their skills and continued their education. The post-literacy campaigns focused on:

• Continuing Education: This stage involved offering further education opportunities for newly literate adults. They were introduced to higher-order reading, writing, and numeracy skills.

• Practical Application of Skills: Adult learners were encouraged to apply their new literacy skills to practical aspects of daily life, such as managing finances, understanding health information, and participating in local governance.

• Retention of Literacy: Literacy tends to decline if it is not actively used, so post-literacy programs included the establishment of libraries, book reading clubs, and continuing education centers to keep learners engaged.

**3. *State-Level Literacy Mission Authorities:*** Each state had its own State Literacy Mission Authority (SLMA) to implement the NLM at the grassroots level. The SLMA coordinated with the central government and local authorities to manage the literacy programs. They were responsible for:

• Planning and implementing literacy campaigns

• Mobilizing resources and volunteers

• Ensuring quality in teaching and learning materials

• Monitoring progress and assessing the outcomes of literacy campaigns.

**Achievements of the National Literacy Mission**

The NLM has had several notable successes:

1. Increase in Literacy Rates: The literacy rate in India increased from 43.57% in 1981 to 64.8% in 2001, and further to 74% by 2011, with much of this progress attributed to the efforts of the NLM. Particularly, the mission succeeded in increasing literacy among women and disadvantaged communities.

2. District-Specific Campaigns: The NLM successfully implemented district-level Total Literacy Campaigns across the country. Many of these campaigns, such as those in Ernakulam (Kerala) and Midnapore (West Bengal), became model literacy programs, influencing literacy efforts across other states.

3. Bridging the Gender Gap: One of the NLM's biggest achievements was the significant increase in female literacy, which had been alarmingly low prior to the mission. By focusing on women, particularly in rural areas, the NLM helped reduce gender disparities in literacy.

4. Creating a Volunteer-Based Education System: The mission's reliance on volunteers, often drawn from the community itself, created a sustainable, cost-effective model for spreading literacy. Many volunteers continued to contribute to literacy efforts even after specific campaigns concluded.

5. Decentralized and Community-Based Approach: The NLM's success was largely due to its community-centric approach. By involving local panchayats, NGOs, and community leaders, the mission ensured that literacy campaigns were rooted in local culture and needs, making them more relevant and impactful. **Benefits of the National Literacy Mission**

1. Economic Growth and Development Literacy is directly linked to economic productivity. As more adults became literate, their ability to engage in skilled labor increased, contributing to economic growth. Educated individuals are also more likely to be employed, start businesses, or improve their existing jobs.

2. Empowerment of Women The NLM had a particular focus on women, recognizing that educating women leads to broader social benefits. Literacy enables women to make informed decisions about health, education, and employment, leading to greater autonomy and family well-being.

3. Improvement in Health and Sanitation Through literacy, individuals gained access to important health and sanitation information, improving their quality of life. Literate adults are better equipped to understand healthcare instructions, hygiene practices, and the importance of vaccination and nutrition, leading to healthier communities.

4. Social and Political Participation Educated individuals are more likely to participate in civic and political activities, such as voting, understanding laws, or engaging in local governance. The NLM enabled millions of individuals to be active participants in India's democracy.

5. Reduction in Population Growth Literacy, particularly among women, is correlated with lower birth rates. Educated women are more likely to be aware of family planning options and the importance of small family sizes, contributing to a reduction in population growth rates.

The National Literacy Mission was a groundbreaking initiative aimed at addressing one of India's most significant challenges—illiteracy. By focusing on adults, especially women and disadvantaged communities, the NLM not only improved literacy rates but also had far-reaching social, economic, and political benefits. The mission empowered individuals by equipping them with functional literacy, thus allowing them to improve their quality of life, contribute to economic growth, and participate fully in the democratic process. Although India still faces challenges related to literacy, the NLM laid a strong foundation for further educational reforms and progress.

### 5.3 Open and Distance Learning

Open and Distance Learning (ODL) refers to a mode of education that allows learners to pursue studies without being physically present in a traditional classroom or campus. It provides flexibility in terms of time, place, and pace of learning, and is particularly beneficial for individuals who cannot attend regular classes due to various personal, professional, or geographical constraints. ODL systems combine open learning—where access is unrestricted and learning is self-paced—with distance education, which uses various technologies to bridge the gap between learners and instructors.

### Meaning of Open and Distance Learning

Open learning is characterized by the absence of barriers related to age, prior qualifications, or time constraints. It provides learners with the freedom to choose what, how, and when they want to study. The "open" aspect focuses on removing constraints such as entry requirements, fixed schedules, or strict completion deadlines. Learning resources are designed to be accessible and adaptable, allowing learners to study at their own convenience.

Distance learning refers to the mode of education where teaching is imparted without the learners being physically present in the same location as the teacher. It utilizes correspondence methods, online platforms, video conferencing, and broadcasting (radio/TV) to deliver education. Unlike conventional classroom learning, where interaction is face-to-face, distance learning enables learners to receive education through remote communication technologies, with little or no physical presence required.

When combined, *ODL* offers learners the opportunity to gain qualifications while balancing other commitments such as work, family, or location constraints. The increasing use of the internet, educational software, and online platforms has revolutionized distance learning, making it a preferred mode of education for millions globally.

### 5.3.1 Need for Open and Distance Learning

*1. Access to Education for All:* One of the primary needs for ODL is to make education accessible to people who are unable to attend conventional institutions. This includes individuals in remote or rural areas, working professionals, people with disabilities, or those who cannot afford to relocate for educational purposes. Example: A young person living in a remote village with no access to universities can pursue a degree from an open university through online courses and virtual classrooms.

*2. Lifelong Learning:* In a rapidly changing world, education is no longer confined to the early stages of life. People need to continually upgrade their skills and knowledge throughout their careers. ODL provides the flexibility to study while continuing to work, making it essential for lifelong learning. Example: A mid-career professional can enroll in a distance learning course to gain a postgraduate qualification in their field without interrupting their job.

*3. Cost-Effective Education:* ODL provides a more affordable alternative to traditional education. With fewer overhead costs such as campus facilities, transportation, and accommodation, ODL institutions can offer quality education at a lower cost. This makes higher education more affordable for a larger population. Example: A person who cannot afford to pay high tuition fees for a regular college course can enroll in an ODL program, saving money while still receiving quality education.

*4. Flexible Learning Environment:* For people with family commitments, jobs, or other personal obligations, ODL offers the flexibility to learn at their own pace and schedule. The flexibility provided by distance learning is one of its major advantages, allowing learners to study at any time and from any location. Example: A mother with small children may find it impossible to attend regular classes but can study for her degree in the evenings when her children are asleep.

*5. Catering to Diverse Learning Needs:* Different learners have different learning styles, and not everyone thrives in a conventional classroom setting. Some learners prefer self-paced study, where they can take the time to grasp concepts deeply. ODL caters to these individual learning needs by offering personalized learning opportunities.

*6. Globalization of Education:* ODL allows institutions to provide education to learners across the globe, breaking down geographical barriers. Learners can access educational opportunities from renowned universities and institutions from anywhere in the world, increasing the internationalization of education. Example: A student in India can enroll in an online course offered by a university in the UK, gaining access to global educational content and certifications.

### 5.3.2 Importance of Open and Distance Learning

1. *Wider Reach and Inclusivity:* ODL is crucial in expanding the reach of education to marginalized and underrepresented groups. Traditional education systems often exclude people due to socio-economic, geographical, or cultural barriers. ODL ensures that these barriers are minimized, providing equal opportunities for education to all. Example: In many developing countries, women are often discouraged from attending regular schools due to cultural norms. ODL provides them with the opportunity to pursue education from home, allowing them to gain qualifications and improve their economic prospects.

2. *Promoting Lifelong Learning and Skill Development:* In today's fast-evolving job market, individuals need to continually update their skills and knowledge. ODL offers professionals and working adults the ability to continue their education without leaving their jobs, making it easier to acquire new qualifications and certifications. Example: An IT professional may need to learn new programming languages or upgrade their skills in cloud computing. They can enroll in online courses and certifications that offer the necessary knowledge without disrupting their career.

3. *Addressing Capacity Constraints in Traditional Systems:* Many countries, particularly those with large populations, face significant challenges in providing enough physical infrastructure and teaching staff to meet the demand for education. ODL addresses these capacity constraints by offering a scalable solution. Example: In India, where universities are overcrowded and many students cannot secure admission, ODL institutions like Indira Gandhi National Open University (IGNOU) provide opportunities for thousands of learners to pursue higher education.

4. *Providing Flexible Learning Pathways:* ODL promotes flexible and customizable learning paths, allowing learners to pace their education according to their personal schedules. This flexibility is particularly important for adult learners who may have work, family, or other responsibilities. Example: A person working in shifts can adjust their study times according to their work schedule, making it easier to balance education with professional commitments.

5. *Bridging the Education Gap in Emergencies:* In times of emergencies like natural disasters, pandemics, or political unrest, traditional education

systems may be disrupted. ODL becomes an invaluable resource to ensure the continuity of education when regular institutions are closed or inaccessible. Example: During the COVID-19 pandemic, millions of students around the world were able to continue their studies through distance learning programs, ensuring that education did not come to a halt despite widespread school closures.

*6. Fostering Self-Motivation and Responsibility:* Distance learning requires students to be more self-disciplined and motivated than in conventional learning environments. Learners must take responsibility for managing their own study schedules, which fosters independence, self-regulation, and time-management skills. Example: A student pursuing an online degree must manage their own time and complete assignments without direct supervision, cultivating skills that are valuable both in academia and the workplace.

*7. Encouraging the Use of Technology in Education:* ODL systems heavily rely on digital platforms, tools, and resources, fostering technological literacy among learners. This promotes the use of e-learning platforms, virtual classrooms, discussion forums, and digital libraries, which prepare students for the modern digital economy. Example: A distance learning program may require students to use educational software, participate in online forums, and access cloud-based resources, thereby enhancing their technological competence.

*8. Supporting Vocational and Professional Development:* ODL plays an essential role in providing vocational and professional courses that focus on skill development. It offers specialized certifications and diplomas in fields such as healthcare, IT, management, and more, helping individuals acquire industry-relevant skills. Example: A healthcare worker looking to specialize in medical coding can enroll in an online certification course that provides the necessary technical training for career advancement.

*9. Promoting Education in Remote and Rural Areas:* Many regions, especially in rural and geographically remote areas, lack access to quality educational institutions. ODL helps bridge this gap by providing access to quality education regardless of location. Example: A student in a remote Himalayan village may not have access to a nearby college but can pursue a degree program through online classes offered by an ODL institution.

### 5.3.3 Role of Open and Distance Learning in India

India has embraced ODL as a critical component of its educational strategy. Institutions such as the Indira Gandhi National Open University

(IGNOU) have been pioneers in providing higher education to millions of learners through open and distance modes. Other universities and private organizations have also adopted ODL, recognizing its potential to reach underserved populations and enhance the nation's educational outcomes.

Key examples of ODL in India include:

· *IGNOU:* With a network of study centers across India, IGNOU is the largest open university in the world, offering undergraduate, postgraduate, and vocational programs to millions of students.

· *State Open Universities:* Several Indian states, including Andhra Pradesh, Maharashtra, and Tamil Nadu, have established their own open universities to cater to regional education needs through distance learning.

Open and Distance Learning (ODL) is a transformative educational approach that addresses the needs of today's diverse learner population. It offers flexibility, affordability, and inclusivity, making education accessible to all—regardless of geographical, social, or economic barriers. ODL fosters lifelong learning, skill development, and professional growth, making it an indispensable tool for individuals and society alike in the globalized, knowledge-driven world. With advancements in digital technology, the potential of ODL will only continue to grow, providing education to more people.

## 5.4 Sailent Features of Distance Education

A Comprehensive Overview

Distance education, also known as distance learning or online learning, is an educational model that allows students to receive instruction and complete coursework without being physically present in a traditional classroom setting. It leverages various forms of technology and communication methods to connect learners with educators, enabling flexible, remote access to education. Distance education is becoming an increasingly popular alternative to traditional education, offering solutions to individuals who face barriers in attending regular, on-campus classes due to geographical, time, or personal constraints. It can be broadly defined as a formal learning process in which the majority of instruction occurs when students and instructors are not in the same location. It allows learners to study independently or with minimal in-person interaction while still receiving structured guidance from teachers or educational institutions. The primary mode of communication is usually technology-based, which can include:

• Online platforms and learning management systems (LMS) like Moodle, Blackboard, or Google Classroom
• Emails and discussion boards
• Video conferencing tools such as Zoom, Google Meet, or Skype
• Pre-recorded video lectures and podcasts
• Study materials sent via mail or online repositories

Distance education is characterized by several key features that distinguish it from traditional forms of education. These features make it accessible, flexible, and effective for a wide range of learners, particularly those unable to participate in conventional classroom-based education. Some of the salient features of distance education are as under:

**1. *Learner-Centered Approach:*** Distance education places the learner at the center of the educational process. Unlike traditional settings where the teacher guides the learning process, distance education emphasizes self-directed learning, allowing students to take responsibility for their studies. Learners can choose the pace, time, and place of their learning, making it adaptable to their personal and professional lives. Example: A working professional pursuing an online degree can study during their free time and adjust their schedule based on personal needs.

**2. *Flexibility in Time and Location:*** One of the most notable features of distance education is its flexibility. Students are not required to attend classes at specific times or locations. They can access course materials, lectures, and assignments whenever and wherever it is convenient for them. This is particularly beneficial for people with busy schedules, full-time jobs, or those living in remote areas. Example: A student in a rural village without access to a local university can still complete a degree program by accessing lectures online.

**3. *Use of Technology for Instruction:*** Distance education heavily relies on technology to facilitate teaching and learning. Tools such as online learning platforms, video conferencing, email, and interactive software are used to deliver course materials, facilitate communication between students and instructors, and provide feedback. The use of multimedia—videos, podcasts, e-books, and digital simulations—enhances the learning experience. Example: Platforms like Moodle or Blackboard allow students to access course materials, submit assignments, and interact with peers and instructors online.

**4. *Asynchronous and Synchronous Learning Options:*** Distance education offers both asynchronous and synchronous learning modes:

• Asynchronous Learning: Students can learn at their own pace without being required to be online at specific times. Lectures, assignments, and discussions can be accessed at any time.

• Synchronous Learning: Live sessions are scheduled where students and instructors interact in real time, often through video conferencing or live chats. Example: A student may watch a pre-recorded lecture (asynchronous learning) but attend a live Q&A session with the professor (synchronous learning).

**5. *Open Admission Policies:*** Most distance education programs have open or flexible admission policies, allowing students from diverse backgrounds and with varying levels of prior education to enroll. This approach lowers traditional barriers to entry, making education accessible to individuals who may not meet stringent admission requirements in traditional universities. Example: Many open universities, like IGNOU (Indira Gandhi National Open University) in India, accept students without the need for entrance exams, providing access to higher education for a broader demographic.

**6. *Self-Paced Learning:*** Distance education allows students to move through the material at their own pace. This feature is particularly beneficial for learners who may need more time to understand complex concepts or who can progress faster through easier material. Self-pacing also accommodates students with other commitments, such as jobs or family responsibilities. Example: An online course might allow students to complete assignments over several weeks, giving them flexibility in managing their study time.

**7. *Cost-Effective Education:*** Distance education is often more cost-effective than traditional education because it eliminates the need for expenses such as commuting, accommodation, and campus facilities. Course fees are generally lower, making it an affordable option for many learners. Example: Students studying through an open university or online platform can avoid relocation and accommodation costs, making higher education more financially accessible.

**8. *Diverse Range of Course Offerings:*** Distance education offers a wide range of courses and programs, including vocational training, undergraduate and postgraduate degrees, professional certifications, and short courses. Students can choose from a variety of subjects and disciplines, from humanities to engineering to business administration. Example: A student can pursue a specialized certificate in digital marketing online while continuing to work full-time.

**9. *Customized and Adaptive Learning:*** Distance education often incorporates adaptive learning technologies that personalize the learning experience based on an individual's progress and needs. This feature allows learners to focus on areas they find challenging and skip sections they have already mastered. Example: Online learning platforms may offer quizzes or assessments that adjust the difficulty level of questions based on the learner's previous responses.

**10. *Global Access and Networking Opportunities:*** Distance education enables students to enroll in programs from universities and institutions across the globe. This creates opportunities to connect with diverse cultures, perspectives, and knowledge systems. Learners are also able to interact with peers from different countries, expanding their professional networks. Example: A student in Africa can enroll in a distance learning program offered by a university in Europe, gaining exposure to international teaching standards and classmates from various regions.

**11. *Support Services for Learners:*** Many distance education institutions provide comprehensive support services to help learners succeed. These services may include access to digital libraries, academic advising, career counseling, technical support, and online tutoring. These support systems ensure that distance learners are not isolated in their studies and have access to necessary resources. Example: A student struggling with a particular subject can receive virtual tutoring or access recorded webinars to reinforce their understanding.

**12. *Assessment and Feedback:*** Assessment methods in distance education are often designed to be flexible and can include online quizzes, assignments, project submissions, and virtual exams. Feedback is usually provided through digital channels, allowing students to monitor their progress and improve continuously. Example: A student might submit an essay electronically and receive detailed feedback from their instructor via email or the online learning platform.

**13. *Minimal Physical Infrastructure Requirements:*** Distance education programs require minimal physical infrastructure, as learning occurs remotely. This feature reduces the costs associated with maintaining physical campuses, classrooms, and other facilities. As a result, it provides an effective solution for education systems with limited resources. Example: A university might offer a full degree program online, using virtual classrooms, without requiring a physical campus.

**14. *Promotes Lifelong Learning:*** Distance education supports the concept of lifelong learning by making education accessible to people at any stage of life. Adults who wish to change careers, acquire new skills, or pursue personal interests can continue learning without the constraints of traditional educational systems. Example: An older adult might take an online course in creative writing to explore a passion that they didn't have time to pursue earlier in life.

**15. *Multimedia and Interactive Content:*** Distance education programs often make use of multimedia to enhance learning, including videos, audio files, interactive simulations, and infographics. This makes the learning experience more engaging and caters to different learning styles. Example: An online science course might include virtual labs where students can conduct experiments using simulations, allowing them to visualize complex scientific processes.

Distance education, with its diverse features, offers an effective and flexible alternative to traditional education. By leveraging technology, providing open access, and fostering learner autonomy, it addresses the needs of various learners—ranging from working professionals to students in remote areas. With growing advancements in online learning technologies, distance education continues to evolve, offering greater opportunities for global access to high-quality education.

## 5.6 Open University System

The *Open University system* is an educational model designed to provide flexible, accessible, and inclusive higher education to a wide range of learners, regardless of their prior academic qualifications or geographic location. This system is characterized by its open admission policies, distance learning methodologies, and a focus on lifelong learning. Open Universities have gained prominence worldwide, offering students the opportunity to pursue higher education without the traditional constraints of time, location, or stringent admission criteria.

*Definition of the Open University System*

An Open University is an institution that offers distance education programs with minimal or no formal entry requirements. It is dedicated to making education more accessible by removing traditional barriers such as previous academic achievement, age, or physical attendance. Open Universities typically use a blend of online learning and self-study materials to deliver courses, allowing students to learn at their own pace and from any location.

Example: The Open University (OU) in the United Kingdom, established in 1969, is a pioneer of this system. It provides degree programs through distance learning and has no formal entry requirements for many courses.

Key Features of the Open University System

*1. Open Admission Policy:* The hallmark of the Open University system is its open-door policy for admissions. Unlike traditional universities that require prior academic qualifications such as high school diplomas or entrance exams, Open Universities often accept learners without these prerequisites. This inclusivity allows individuals from diverse educational and professional backgrounds to enroll in courses and degree programs.

Example: A person without a high school diploma can still enroll in an undergraduate program at many Open Universities, provided they demonstrate the ability to complete the course.

*2. Distance Learning:* Open Universities primarily operate on a distance learning model, allowing students to access course materials, attend virtual lectures, and complete assessments online or through mailed study materials. This method eliminates the need for students to be physically present on a campus, making education accessible to people in remote or underserved regions.

Example: Students in rural areas can complete degrees offered by Open Universities without needing to travel or relocate to a city.

*3. Flexible Learning Schedule:* The Open University system provides flexibility in terms of learning schedules. Students can typically decide when to start, pause, or complete their courses. This feature is particularly beneficial for working adults, parents, or those with other responsibilities, as it allows them to balance education with personal and professional commitments.

Example: A working professional can complete an MBA degree through an Open University, studying part-time after work hours or on weekends.

*4. Modular and Credit-Based Learning:* Open Universities often offer modular courses, where students can earn credits for each completed module. These credits can be accumulated over time, allowing students to gradually work toward a full qualification at their own pace. This feature supports lifelong learning, as students can return to their studies after breaks.

Example: A student might complete a few modules toward a Bachelor's degree over a few years while balancing a job, and continue completing the remaining modules at a later time.

*5. Self-Directed Learning:* The system emphasizes self-directed learning, requiring students to take responsibility for their study schedules and pace. Though support from tutors and mentors is provided, the focus is on students managing their own education.

Example: Students are given access to study materials and are expected to work through them independently, submitting assignments or taking exams according to the deadlines.

*6. Use of Technology for Education:* Open Universities heavily rely on technology for course delivery, student interaction, and assessments. This includes online learning platforms, discussion forums, virtual classrooms, video lectures, and digital libraries. In many cases, these platforms also provide tools for students to interact with peers and instructors.

Example: An Open University might use platforms like Moodle or Blackboard to deliver course content, while also hosting live webinars or discussion forums for student-teacher interactions.

*7. Cost-Effective Education:* Open Universities are often more affordable than traditional universities, as they do not require the same infrastructure, such as physical campuses, classrooms, or residential facilities. The ability to study from home also reduces costs associated with commuting, relocation, and accommodation.

Example: A student studying online through an Open University avoids costs associated with living on campus, making education more affordable.

*8. Focus on Lifelong Learning:* Open Universities cater to a wide range of learners, including adults seeking to enhance their skills or qualifications later in life. By removing age and qualification barriers, these institutions promote lifelong learning, encouraging individuals to continue their education at any stage in life.

Example: A 50-year-old professional might decide to pursue a degree through an Open University to advance their career or switch to a new field.

**Importance and Benefits of the Open University System**

*1. Access to Higher Education for All:* The Open University system democratizes education by providing opportunities to people who might otherwise be excluded from traditional education systems. It serves those who may not have completed high school, live in remote areas, or have personal or professional responsibilities that prevent them from attending regular universities. Example: A person living in a small village with no nearby university can still obtain a university degree by enrolling in an Open University.

*2. Flexibility for Working Adults:* Open Universities are particularly beneficial for adults who want to pursue higher education without leaving their jobs. The system's flexibility allows students to study part-time or at their own pace while continuing their careers. Example: A nurse might take online courses in healthcare management through an Open University while continuing to work full-time at a hospital.

*3. Inclusion of Non-Traditional Learners:* Open Universities cater to non-traditional learners, including adult learners, people with disabilities, or those who cannot attend full-time, on-campus programs due to personal commitments. This inclusivity helps reduce inequalities in access to education. Example: A person with a disability that prevents them from physically attending a traditional university can complete a degree through distance learning at an Open University.

*4. Affordability:* The lower cost of education in Open Universities makes higher education more accessible to those from lower-income backgrounds. Additionally, students save on costs associated with accommodation and commuting since they can study from home. Example: A student in a developing country can pursue a degree through an Open University without the high costs associated with relocating to a major city for education.

*5. Lifelong Learning and Career Advancement:* Open Universities offer courses for professional development and skill enhancement, which are critical for career advancement. As industries evolve and new skills are required, working professionals can take short courses or diploma programs to stay competitive in the job market. Example: A software engineer might enroll in an online course on machine learning through an Open University to stay updated with the latest technologies.

Examples of Notable Open Universities

1. The Open University (UK): Established in 1969, it is the most famous Open University and offers a wide range of undergraduate and postgraduate programs through distance learning. It has no entry requirements for many programs, and students from around the world can enroll. Example: A student from any country can earn a degree in business administration through The Open University without attending on-campus classes.

2. Indira Gandhi National Open University (IGNOU) – India: Established in 1985, IGNOU is one of the largest Open Universities in the world, offering diverse courses across various disciplines. It plays a crucial role in providing

affordable education to millions of students, especially in rural India. Example: A farmer in India can complete a degree in agricultural sciences through IGNOU's distance education programs without needing to leave their home.

3. The Open University of Sri Lanka: This institution provides a range of programs for students unable to access traditional universities. It uses both distance learning and a limited number of face-to-face interactions to ensure learners can study at their own pace.

4. Athabasca University (Canada): Athabasca University is a leading institution in distance education in North America, providing accessible and flexible degree programs to learners across Canada and internationally.

# VI
## Value Education and Environmental Education

Value Education and Environmental Education are closely linked, both aiming to shape the mindset and behavior of individuals for the betterment of society and the environment. It focuses on instilling moral, ethical, cultural, and social values in individuals to develop a well-rounded personality. It includes teaching compassion, respect, honesty, responsibility, and tolerance. And the aim is to help individuals become responsible citizens and cultivate a sense of empathy, respect for others, and integrity in personal and professional life. Value education is often incorporated through storytelling, discussions, ethical dilemmas, case studies, and role-playing, creating opportunities for students to reflect on their own behavior and that of others.

*Environmental Education* is a process that helps individuals understand the natural environment and the impact human activities have on it. It equips learners with the knowledge, skills, and values needed to address environmental challenges and promote sustainability, and the primary aim is to foster a deeper understanding of environmental issues like pollution, climate change, biodiversity loss, and resource conservation, encouraging individuals to adopt eco-friendly lifestyles.

*Environmental education* is imparted through hands-on activities, field trips, ecological projects, recycling programs, and discussions about current environmental issues. It emphasizes critical thinking and problem-solving skills.

Value education and environmental education often intersect, especially in fostering values like responsibility, respect for nature, sustainability, and community well-being. For instance, teaching students the value of conserving resources directly impacts their behavior toward the environment. Together, these forms of education aim to create a conscientious and informed citizenry capable of making ethical and sustainable choices. Both are vital in shaping a society that values both human well-being and environmental stewardship.

## 6.1 Human Values

*Meaning of Human Values*

Human values are the principles, standards, or qualities that guide individuals in their decision-making processes and behavior, contributing to their overall moral and ethical framework. These values reflect what is fundamentally important in life and help shape personal conduct, interpersonal relationships, and societal norms. Human values are often universal in nature, transcending cultural, social, and geographical boundaries, though they can manifest differently depending on context.

Values like *truth, compassion, respect, justice, responsibility, and honesty* are examples of core human values that play a crucial role in individual and social development. They foster harmony, promote ethical behavior, and help individuals contribute meaningfully to the welfare of society.

Concept of Human Values by Educationists:

In the Words of Mahatma Gandhi (1869-1948): : *"True education should aim at drawing out the best in the child's body, mind, and spirit."*

Gandhi believed that human values, such as truth, non-violence, and self-discipline, are essential components of education. He argued that education is not just about imparting knowledge but also about developing character and fostering a spirit of service to humanity. For Gandhi, values like truth and non-violence (Satyagraha) were fundamental to achieving personal and collective growth.

As John Dewey (1859-1952) defines *"Education is not preparation for life; education is life itself."*

Dewey viewed education as an ongoing process through which individuals continuously engage with their environment, learning to develop human values such as cooperation, democracy, and problem-solving skills. He emphasized experiential learning and critical thinking, believing that human values are cultivated through active participation in a community. For Dewey, values were not abstract ideals but practical tools for living harmoniously within society.

According to Swami Vivekananda (1863-1902) *"Education is the manifestation of the perfection already in man."*

Vivekananda held that education should bring out the inherent potential within individuals, especially focusing on spiritual and moral growth. He stressed values like compassion, selflessness, and dedication to serving others. According to him, the highest purpose of education is to build character, develop self-confidence, and foster a spirit of altruism and social responsibility.

Rabindranath Tagore (1861-1941) believed *"The highest education is that which does not merely give us information but makes our life in harmony with all existence."*

Tagore believed in holistic education that integrates the development of moral, aesthetic, and intellectual faculties. He emphasized the importance of nature, art, and human relationships in education, advocating values like freedom, creativity, and respect for diversity. He saw human values as being essential for individuals to live in harmony with nature and society.

Jiddu Krishnamurti (1895-1986) had a view that *"The function of education is to help you from childhood not to imitate anybody, but to be yourself all the time."*

Krishnamurti's philosophy of education centered around the development of a free and independent mind. He encouraged learners to question societal norms and cultivate values like self-awareness, compassion, and inner freedom. He rejected conformity and believed that real education should foster an understanding of the self and the world, leading to meaningful personal transformation.

Immanuel Kant (1724-1804) defines *"Act only according to that maxim whereby you can at the same time will that it should become a universal law."*

Kant's famous categorical imperative is central to his ethical philosophy. For Kant, values like duty, justice, and moral autonomy are critical. He believed that human beings should act based on principles that could be universally applied, meaning that moral actions should not be based on self-interest but on a sense of duty and respect for others' inherent dignity. Education, therefore, should teach individuals to act ethically and to recognize the inherent value of others.

**Key Human Values in Education:**

*1. Respect:* Recognizing and appreciating the rights, beliefs, and properties of others, and treating them with courtesy and kindness.

*2. Responsibility:* Being accountable for one's actions, fulfilling duties, and making ethical choices in personal and professional life.

*3. Compassion:* Demonstrating empathy and concern for the well-being of others, and being willing to help and support those in need.

*4. Honesty:* Being truthful, sincere, and free of deceit in all interactions.

*5. Justice:* Ensuring fairness, equity, and impartiality in decisions and actions, both at an individual and societal level.

*6. Integrity:* Maintaining consistency in moral principles and standing firm on ethical grounds, regardless of circumstances.

**The Role of Education in Cultivating Human Values:**

Educationists agree that human values should be an integral part of education. Values-based education helps individuals grow as morally conscious and socially responsible members of society. It goes beyond academic achievement to ensure that learners develop a sense of empathy, social awareness, and ethical conduct. Incorporating value education into the curriculum can lead to the following benefits:

• Character Building: It helps develop integrity, self-discipline, and respect for others.

• Social Cohesion: Value education promotes respect for diversity, reducing conflicts and fostering understanding.

• Ethical Leadership: It encourages individuals to become responsible leaders, guided by moral principles.

• Environmental Awareness: Education on values like sustainability fosters a sense of responsibility toward protecting the environment.

Human values are at the core of education, nurturing holistic growth and preparing individuals to contribute positively to the world.

**6.1.1 Need and Importance of Human Values**

Human values are fundamental principles that guide our behavior, interactions, and decision-making. They are essential not just for personal development but also for the well-being of society as a whole. These values, which include respect, responsibility, empathy, compassion, and integrity, play a crucial role in shaping a harmonious, productive, and ethically sound community. Below is an in-depth explanation of the need and importance of human values in various dimensions of life.

**Need for Human Values:**

*1. Foundation of Ethical Behavior:* Human values are the foundation of ethical conduct. They guide individuals in making morally sound decisions and help distinguish between right and wrong. In the absence of values, people may act based solely on self-interest, leading to unethical behavior and harm to others.

*2. Personal Development:* Values such as honesty, compassion, and integrity are integral to an individual's personal growth. They help shape character, develop self-discipline, and foster a sense of responsibility. Human values enable individuals to lead a balanced life, where material success is complemented by emotional and moral well-being.

*3. Social Harmony and Peace:* Human values are essential for fostering peace, cooperation, and understanding in society. Values like tolerance, empathy, and respect help bridge cultural, social, and religious differences. They promote peaceful coexistence and reduce conflicts, as individuals learn to appreciate diversity and work toward common goals.

*4. Strengthening Relationships:* Human values form the bedrock of healthy relationships. Values such as trust, loyalty, and respect strengthen bonds between family members, friends, and colleagues. In the absence of these values, relationships can deteriorate, leading to misunderstandings, conflicts, and social fragmentation.

*5. Building Ethical Leadership:* Leaders who are grounded in human values are more likely to inspire trust, loyalty, and cooperation from their followers. Ethical leadership, rooted in values such as justice, fairness, and responsibility, is crucial for good governance and effective decision-making. Without values, leadership can become corrupt and exploitative.

*6. Global Challenges:* In a world facing numerous global challenges—climate change, inequality, poverty—human values like sustainability, empathy, and social justice are critical. These values drive individuals and societies to take action in the interest of the global community, encouraging responsible consumption, conservation of resources, and equitable distribution of wealth.

*7. Promoting Justice and Equality:* Human values like justice and equality are essential for ensuring that all individuals are treated fairly and have access to opportunities. A value-driven society works towards reducing disparities and injustices, ensuring that marginalized groups are protected and empowered. In this way, human values form the moral backbone of legal and social systems.

*8. Mental and Emotional Well-being:* Values such as contentment, gratitude, and compassion are closely linked to mental health. They provide individuals with a sense of purpose and fulfillment, helping them cope with life's challenges. The absence of values can lead to feelings of emptiness, anxiety, and dissatisfaction, as individuals may pursue material success at the expense of emotional well-being.

**Importance of Human Values:**

*1. Guiding Principles for Life:* Human values serve as guiding principles that influence every aspect of life, from personal choices to professional conduct. They help individuals make consistent and ethical decisions, ensuring that their actions align with their moral beliefs. Without a clear set of values, people can easily lose direction and engage in behavior that may harm themselves or others.

*2. Creating a Moral Framework for Society:* Societies built on a strong foundation of human values are more likely to be just, inclusive, and harmonious. Human values help create a moral framework that governs how people interact with one another, ensuring that basic rights are respected and that individuals are treated with dignity and fairness. They also shape laws, policies, and institutions that protect the vulnerable and promote equality.

*3. Supporting Social Responsibility:* In a world that is increasingly interconnected, human values like empathy and responsibility encourage individuals to contribute to the welfare of their communities and the environment. Value-based education helps foster a sense of social responsibility, urging individuals to take actions that benefit society, such as volunteering, helping the less fortunate, and advocating for social change.

*4. Fostering a Positive Work Environment:* Human values play a crucial role in the professional sphere, fostering trust, collaboration, and accountability. A workplace grounded in values such as integrity, fairness, and respect tends to be more productive, innovative, and inclusive. Employees are more likely to be satisfied and motivated when they are part of an ethical organization that prioritizes human dignity over profit.

*5. Addressing Ethical Dilemmas:* Life is full of complex decisions, and human values are essential for navigating ethical dilemmas. Values like honesty, compassion, and responsibility help individuals weigh the consequences of their actions and make decisions that benefit the greater good. In situations where rules and regulations are unclear, values provide a moral compass to guide behavior.

*6. Preventing Corruption and Exploitation:* Values like justice and integrity are essential for preventing corruption, exploitation, and abuse of power. In the absence of human values, individuals may prioritize personal gain over the well-being of others, leading to unethical practices in business, politics, and daily life. By promoting transparency and fairness, human values help build a more just and equitable society.

*7. Inculcating Civic Virtue:* Civic virtues, such as respect for the law, commitment to public service, and active participation in democratic processes, are underpinned by human values. These values encourage individuals to contribute to the common good, take responsibility for their actions, and work towards creating a better society for all. Value-driven citizens are more likely to vote, volunteer, and engage in activities that promote social justice and equity.

*8. Promoting Environmental Stewardship:* Human values are increasingly recognized as being critical to environmental sustainability. Values like respect for nature, responsibility for future generations, and stewardship of the earth encourage individuals to adopt eco-friendly lifestyles and support environmental policies. Without these values, environmental degradation and resource exploitation can accelerate, leading to long-term harm for humanity.

**Integration of Human Values into Education:**

To emphasize the need for human values in contemporary life, many educationists stress the importance of incorporating value-based education into school curricula. This helps cultivate ethical reasoning, critical thinking, and a sense of moral responsibility from a young age. Schools, families, and communities all play a role in shaping the values of individuals.

• Moral Education: Encouraging students to reflect on ethical issues, understand the consequences of their actions, and make decisions based on fairness and compassion.

• Civic Education: Teaching the importance of citizenship, democracy, and social justice to create informed and engaged citizens.

• Character Education: Helping students develop virtues like resilience, perseverance, and self-control, which are essential for personal success and societal well-being.

Human values are the cornerstones of a well-functioning society. They guide personal behavior, strengthen social bonds, foster ethical leadership, and contribute to global sustainability. Without human values, individuals and societies may pursue short-term gains at the expense of long-term well-being. As the world faces increasingly complex challenges, the need for human values is more critical than ever in building a just, compassionate, and responsible global community.

## 6.2.0 Classification, Development and Inclusion of Human Values

Classification of human values is essential for recognizing their role in personal development, social interaction and global citizenship. By categorizing values, individuals can better comprehend their significance and work toward incorporating them into daily life.

### 1. Personal Values

Personal values are the individual beliefs and principles that shape one's character and influence decisions. They are often the result of personal experiences, reflections, and upbringing.

**Characteristics:**

• Individualistic: Personal values can vary significantly from person to person based on life experiences and choices.

• Intrinsic: They often reflect what an individual considers important in their own life, guiding personal behavior and self-concept.

• Integrity: Upholding honesty and moral principles in all actions.

• Self-discipline: The ability to control impulses and stay focused on long-term goals.

• Courage: The willingness to confront fear, challenges, or adversity.

• Compassion: Showing empathy and concern for the suffering of others.

• Ambition: The desire to achieve personal goals and aspirations.

**Significance:**

• Personal values play a crucial role in defining identity and self-worth. They influence motivation, decision-making, and the overall direction of one's life.

• They contribute to resilience and self-fulfillment, as individuals who live according to their values often experience greater life satisfaction.

### 2. Social Values

Social values govern how individuals interact with each other and contribute to the community. They promote social cohesion and a sense of belonging.

**Characteristics:**

• Collective: Social values are often shared among groups and communities.

• Interpersonal: They focus on the relationships between individuals and how they engage with society.

• Respect: Valuing others' opinions, rights, and dignity, regardless of differences.

• Cooperation: Working collaboratively with others to achieve common goals.

• Empathy: Understanding and being sensitive to the feelings and experiences of others.

• Social Justice: Advocating for fairness and equality for all members of society.

**Significance:**

• Social values are essential for fostering a sense of community and mutual respect. They help mitigate conflicts and build trust among individuals.

• A society rich in social values tends to have lower rates of crime and violence and higher levels of social engagement and civic responsibility.

**3. Moral or Ethical Values**

Moral values are concerned with right and wrong and guide individuals in ethical decision-making. They often stem from cultural, religious, or philosophical traditions.

**Characteristics:**

• Normative: Moral values establish standards for behavior, dictating what is considered right or wrong.

• Universal: While interpretations may vary, many moral values are recognized across different cultures.

• Justice: Ensuring fair treatment and equality in all interactions.

• Honesty: Being truthful and transparent in communication and actions.

• Responsibility: Acknowledging the consequences of one's actions and fulfilling obligations.

• Fairness: Treating others with impartiality and respect.

**Significance:**

• Moral values provide a framework for ethical behavior, helping individuals navigate dilemmas and make choices that align with societal expectations.

• They contribute to a functioning legal system and promote trust and cooperation in society.

**4. Cultural or Religious Values**

Cultural and religious values are derived from specific traditions, customs, and beliefs that shape a group's identity and practices. These values influence behavior and norms within a particular cultural or religious context.

**Characteristics**:

• Contextual: They are often deeply rooted in historical and cultural contexts.

• Prescriptive: Cultural and religious values provide guidelines for behavior and lifestyle choices.

• Family Loyalty: Valuing family connections and obligations, often emphasized in many cultures.

• Charity: The moral obligation to assist those in need, which is common in many religions.

• Tradition: Upholding customs and practices that are significant to cultural identity.

• Spiritual Growth: The pursuit of personal enlightenment and connection with a higher power.

**Significance:**

• Cultural and religious values help individuals understand their place in the world and contribute to social cohesion within communities.

• They can also promote tolerance and understanding among different groups when individuals appreciate diverse traditions and practices.

**5. Universal Values** Universal values are principles that are recognized and upheld across different cultures and societies. They transcend local traditions and are often associated with global human rights.

**Characteristics:**

• Global: Universal values are applicable to all people, regardless of cultural, social, or economic backgrounds.

• Fundamental: They are often seen as essential for the well-being and dignity of all individuals.

• Peace: The absence of conflict and the promotion of harmony among individuals and nations.

• Human Rights: Recognition of the basic rights and freedoms inherent to all individuals.

• Sustainability: The responsibility to protect the environment for future generations.

• Equality: The belief that all individuals should have the same rights and opportunities.

**Significance:**

• Universal values are critical for addressing global challenges, such as poverty, inequality, and environmental issues. They promote a sense of shared responsibility among nations and individuals.

• They serve as guiding principles for international law and global governance, fostering cooperation and understanding among diverse peoples.

**Interconnections Among Classifications**

• Personal and Social Values: Personal values often influence social values. For instance, an individual's commitment to honesty (personal value) can foster a culture of transparency and trust in their community (social value).

• Moral and Cultural Values: Moral values can be influenced by cultural and religious teachings, shaping what is deemed acceptable behavior in a given society.

• Universal Values and All Classifications: Universal values can act as a unifying framework that connects personal, social, moral, and cultural values, promoting a holistic understanding of human dignity and rights.

Understanding the classification of human values is essential for recognizing their diverse roles in shaping individual behavior, societal interactions, and global citizenship. Each classification serves a unique purpose, contributing to personal growth, social harmony, ethical conduct, and cultural identity. By fostering a deeper appreciation of these values, individuals can work toward building more compassionate, just, and sustainable communities.

**6.2.1 Development of Human Values**

The development of human values is a complex and dynamic process influenced by various factors throughout an individual's life. Understanding how these values are formed, shaped, and modified can help in promoting positive behavior and fostering a more ethical society. A detailed exploration of the development of human values:

**1. Early Childhood Development**

• Family Influence : Primary Source of Values is the family unit is often the first place where children are introduced to values. Parents, siblings, and other family members model behaviors and attitudes that children observe and internalize.

• Communication of Values: Through discussions, stories, and daily interactions, families communicate values like respect, kindness, responsibility, and honesty. For instance, a child learns about sharing and cooperation by observing family members during mealtimes or play.

• Emotional Climate: The emotional environment within the family (e.g., warmth, support, and open communication) significantly impacts the development of empathy, trust, and other social values. Learning through Observation includes:

• Role Modeling: Children learn by imitating the behavior of adults. If parents demonstrate compassion and honesty, children are more likely to adopt these values.

• Reinforcement: Positive reinforcement for exhibiting desirable behaviors (like praising a child for helping others) strengthens value development.

## 2. Educational Environment

Formal Education involve Value-Based Education: Schools play a crucial role in reinforcing and expanding upon the values taught at home. Many educational systems incorporate moral education, character education, and social-emotional learning into their curricula.

• Discussion and Reflection: Classroom discussions about ethical dilemmas, literature with moral themes, and historical events can prompt students to reflect on their values and understand diverse perspectives.

• Extracurricular Activities: Participation in sports, clubs, and community service projects can cultivate values such as teamwork, leadership, and social responsibility.

Peer Influence which include:

• Social Dynamics: As children grow, peers become increasingly influential in value development. Friendships and social interactions introduce new values and challenge existing ones. •

Group Norms: The values upheld by peer groups can significantly affect an individual's behavior. For example, a peer group that values academic achievement may encourage its members to adopt similar priorities.

## 3. Cultural and Societal Factors

Cultural Influences and Cultural Heritage: Values are often deeply embedded in cultural practices, traditions, and rituals. Cultural celebrations, customs, and religious practices can instill values such as respect for elders, community service, and environmental stewardship.

• Diverse Perspectives: Exposure to different cultures can broaden one's understanding of values. Learning about the values of other cultures fosters tolerance, empathy, and a global perspective. Social Norms and Media

• Mass Media: Television, movies, literature, and social media can influence the formation of values. They often depict scenarios that highlight specific values, shaping public perceptions of what is important or desirable.

• Public Discourse: Social movements, political discourse, and community discussions also play a role in shaping values. For instance, movements advocating for human rights and social justice can promote values such as equality and fairness.

### 4. Personal Experiences and Reflections Life Experiences

• Critical Life Events: Significant life experiences, such as overcoming adversity, loss, or success, can lead to profound shifts in values. For example, someone who experiences hardship may develop a stronger sense of empathy and compassion for others facing similar challenges.

• Travel and Exposure: Traveling and interacting with diverse populations can challenge preconceived notions and broaden one's understanding of human values, leading to personal growth and value reassessment.

• Introspection (Self-Reflection): Individuals often engage in self-reflection, questioning their beliefs and values. This process can be prompted by life changes, education, or exposure to new ideas.

• Value Alignment: People may reassess their values based on personal experiences and the alignment of their actions with their beliefs. This reflection helps individuals develop a more coherent and authentic value system.

### 5. Continuous Development Throughout Life

Lifelong Learning an Ongoing Process: Value development is not confined to childhood or adolescence; it continues throughout adulthood as individuals encounter new experiences and perspectives.

• Adaptation: As society evolves, individuals may need to adapt their values in response to changing norms, technological advancements, and global challenges. For example, growing awareness of environmental issues may lead to the adoption of more sustainable values.

• Mentorship and Role Models which means Influence of Leaders: Mentors, teachers, and community leaders can influence the development of values by providing guidance and serving as role models. Their actions and words can inspire individuals to embody similar values.

• Community Engagement: Participation in community service or activism can further reinforce values of empathy, social responsibility, and justice. Engaging with diverse groups helps individuals appreciate different perspectives and develop inclusive values.

## 6. Institutional Influence Religious and Spiritual Institutions

• Religious Teachings: For many individuals, religious institutions play a vital role in shaping values. Religious teachings often emphasize moral behavior, community service, and compassion.

• Spiritual Growth: Spiritual practices can promote reflection and personal growth, encouraging individuals to develop values related to forgiveness, gratitude, and humility.

• Workplace Culture & Corporate Values: The culture of an organization can shape employees' values and behaviors. Companies that prioritize ethical practices and social responsibility foster a work environment that aligns with those values.

• Professional Development: Training programs that emphasize ethical decision-making, diversity, and inclusion can help employees develop and refine their values in a professional context.

The development of human values is a multifaceted process influenced by family, education, culture, personal experiences, and social interactions. Values are not static; they evolve as individuals grow, learn, and adapt to new experiences and challenges. By fostering environments that promote value development—whether at home, in schools, workplaces, or communities—we can encourage individuals to embody values that contribute to personal fulfillment, social harmony, and a more just and equitable world. Understanding this developmental process is crucial for educators, parents, and community leaders who aim to nurture positive values in individuals and society.

### 6.2.2 Inclusion of Human Values

The inclusion of human values refers to the intentional integration of values such as empathy, respect, honesty, responsibility, and justice into various aspects of life—whether in personal development, educational systems, workplaces, communities, or societal structures. This inclusion aims to foster an environment where ethical behavior and positive relationships thrive, ultimately contributing to the well-being of individuals and society. Below is how human values can be included and promoted in different domains:

### 1. Inclusion of Human Values in Education

Curriculum Integration

• Value-Based Education: Including human values in the educational curriculum is a crucial strategy to instill ethics and moral reasoning in students. Subjects such as social studies, literature, philosophy, and religious education can be used to explore concepts like fairness, empathy, and social responsibility.

• Character Education Programs: Many schools adopt specific programs designed to teach character and values. These programs focus on core values such as honesty, integrity, respect for others, and responsibility.

• Moral Dilemmas: Including discussions about moral dilemmas and ethical decision-making in classrooms encourages students to critically think about values and their application in real-life situations.

Role of Teachers

• Teachers as Role Models: Educators play a vital role in including human values by demonstrating them in their interactions with students. Teachers who act with fairness, compassion, and integrity inspire students to adopt similar behaviors.

• Encouraging Respectful Behavior: Teachers can promote values like respect, cooperation, and kindness by creating a classroom environment that encourages positive interactions, collaboration, and mutual support.

• Service Learning: Involving students in community service or service-learning projects is an effective way to include values such as empathy, social responsibility, and altruism in their education. These projects allow students to connect classroom learning with real-world applications of human values.

## 2. Inclusion of Human Values in Family Life

Parental Guidance

• Leading by Example: Parents and caregivers are the primary source of value education for children. When parents demonstrate honesty, respect, empathy, and responsibility in their own behavior, children are more likely to adopt these values.

• Open Communication: Encouraging open discussions about values, ethics, and decision-making helps children understand the importance of these principles in everyday life.

• Instilling Responsibility: Involving children in household chores, decision-making, and family responsibilities helps them develop values such as accountability, discipline, and respect for others' contributions.

Daily Practices

• Routine Reinforcement: Establishing family traditions or routines, such as showing gratitude at meals or engaging in acts of kindness, can reinforce values over time.

• Conflict Resolution: Families can teach values like tolerance, patience, and empathy by modeling constructive conflict resolution methods, emphasizing listening, understanding, and compromise.

### 3. Inclusion of Human Values in the Workplace

Organizational Culture

• Ethical Leadership: Companies and organizations that prioritize ethical leadership foster a culture where human values are embedded in daily operations. Leaders who demonstrate integrity, fairness, and respect encourage employees to adopt similar behaviors.

• Corporate Social Responsibility (CSR): Many companies include human values in their corporate strategies by adopting CSR practices, focusing on environmental sustainability, fair labor practices, and community outreach programs. This aligns business practices with broader values like justice, equity, and care for the environment.

• Value-Based Decision Making: Encouraging value-based decision-making, where decisions are evaluated not only based on profit but also on their ethical implications, helps create a more values-driven organization.

Diversity and Inclusion

• Promoting Respect for Diversity: Workplaces that prioritize diversity and inclusion actively embrace the values of equality, fairness, and respect for different cultures, perspectives, and backgrounds. This inclusion fosters a sense of belonging and ensures all employees feel valued and respected.

• Employee Development: Providing training and professional development focused on ethical behavior, leadership, and interpersonal skills can help employees integrate human values into their professional roles.

### 4. Inclusion of Human Values in Society and Governance

Policy and Legislation

• Human Rights Laws: Governments can include human values in society by enacting and enforcing laws that protect human rights, promote equality, and ensure justice for all citizens. These laws reflect the values of fairness, equality, and respect for individual dignity.

• Social Welfare Programs: Policies that aim to reduce poverty, ensure access to education, healthcare, and basic needs are grounded in the values of compassion, social justice, and equity.

• Environmental Protection: Governments and organizations that promote sustainability and environmental protection demonstrate values like responsibility, stewardship, and intergenerational fairness, ensuring that future generations have the resources they need.

Community and Civic Engagement

• Promoting Volunteerism: Encouraging civic engagement and volunteerism helps to promote values such as empathy, service to others, and a sense of community. When individuals volunteer in local shelters, schools, or hospitals, they actively contribute to a society built on mutual respect and kindness.

• Inclusive Communities: Communities that value inclusivity, diversity, and mutual support create environments where individuals feel accepted, respected, and empowered. These communities often engage in initiatives that promote cultural understanding, social justice, and equity for marginalized groups.

**5. Inclusion of Human Values in Personal Development**

Self-Reflection and Growth

• Mindfulness and Reflection: Personal practices such as mindfulness, journaling, or meditation can foster self-awareness and reflection on one's values. By regularly considering how their actions align with their values, individuals can strive to live more ethical and fulfilling lives.

• Learning from Experience: Life experiences, especially challenges and conflicts, offer opportunities for individuals to reflect on their values and grow. By learning from mistakes and striving to be better, individuals develop resilience, empathy, and integrity.

• Goal-Setting Aligned with Values: Individuals can include human values in their personal growth by setting life goals that are aligned with ethical principles, such as helping others, contributing to society, or pursuing fairness and justice.

Continuous Learning

• Education Beyond School: Personal development programs, such as workshops on emotional intelligence, ethical leadership, or community building, can help individuals integrate human values into their lives. These programs emphasize personal growth, empathy, and the importance of ethical behavior in all areas of life.

• Mentorship and Role Models: Having mentors or role models who embody strong human values provides individuals with examples of how to include values like honesty, integrity, and fairness in their personal and professional lives.

**6. Inclusion of Human Values in Global Initiatives**

International Cooperation

• Humanitarian Aid and Development: Global organizations, such as the United Nations or international NGOs, often promote values like compassion, justice, and equality by supporting humanitarian efforts, such as poverty alleviation, disaster relief, and healthcare access.

• Climate Action: Efforts to combat climate change and protect the environment reflect a global commitment to values like sustainability, responsibility, and respect for future generations.

Global Education Initiatives

• Promoting Universal Values: Educational programs aimed at fostering peace, equality, and global citizenship work to include universal human values in the curriculum, helping individuals across the world embrace values that transcend cultural differences.

• Cultural Exchange: Initiatives that promote cultural exchange and understanding, such as student exchange programs or international collaboration, encourage the inclusion of values like tolerance, empathy, and respect for diversity.

The inclusion of human values in various areas of life is essential for fostering a more compassionate, just, and responsible society. From early childhood education to workplace culture, from personal development to global initiatives, values like empathy, fairness, and responsibility shape the way we interact with the world and each other. By intentionally integrating these values into all aspects of life, individuals and institutions can contribute to a more ethical, inclusive, and harmonious society.

## 6.3 Environmental Education

Environmental education is the process of teaching and learning about the environment, its challenges, and the ways humans can sustainably interact with it. The goal is to increase awareness, develop knowledge, and foster attitudes and behaviors that promote environmental protection and stewardship.

### Concept of Environmental Education

Environmental education (EE) is a multidisciplinary approach that integrates various fields like biology, ecology, geography, chemistry, and social sciences to provide a holistic understanding of the environment. The concept goes beyond merely imparting knowledge about the natural world. It encourages individuals and communities to become actively involved in protecting the environment and making informed decisions to solve environmental problems. EE addresses complex environmental issues such as climate change, deforestation, pollution, resource depletion, and biodiversity loss, empowering individuals to adopt sustainable practices and contribute to the well-being of the planet.

**Meaning and Key Components**

Environmental education involves several key components that guide its implementation and practice:

**1. Awareness and Sensitivity to the Environment**

• Awareness: EE helps individuals recognize the importance of the environment in sustaining life and well-being. It aims to cultivate an understanding of both local and global environmental issues.

• Sensitivity: It fosters emotional connections to the environment, encouraging people to care about nature and recognize the urgency of environmental conservation.

**2. Knowledge and Understanding**

• Scientific Understanding: Environmental education provides a scientific foundation about natural ecosystems, environmental processes, and human impacts on the planet. It helps individuals comprehend how the environment functions and how various factors (e.g., human activities) influence it.

• Interconnectedness: It teaches that the environment is interconnected with social, economic, and political systems. Environmental problems do not occur in isolation, and solving them requires a multidisciplinary approach.

**3. Attitudes and Values**

• Fostering Responsibility: EE helps develop ethical attitudes toward the environment, encouraging individuals to respect nature and take responsibility for its preservation.

• Value Systems: It aims to instill values like sustainability, conservation, and equity, influencing individuals to make decisions that balance environmental health with human needs.

**4. Skills for Solving Environmental Problems**

• Critical Thinking: EE develops problem-solving skills by encouraging students to critically analyze environmental issues and propose viable solutions.

• Practical Skills: Learners acquire practical skills, such as waste management, energy conservation, water conservation, and sustainable agricultural practices, which they can apply in daily life to minimize their environmental footprint.

**5. Participation and Action**

• Active Engagement: Environmental education promotes active participation in local and global environmental initiatives. It encourages students and communities to engage in conservation activities, policy advocacy, and sustainable practices.

• Empowerment: It empowers individuals to take action to protect the environment and contribute to sustainable development, whether by changing personal habits, participating in community efforts, or influencing policies.

### 6.3.1 Nature Of Environmental Education

The nature of environmental education is characterized by its interdisciplinary approach, its focus on fostering awareness and responsibility, and its emphasis on active participation and problem-solving. It aims to cultivate a deep understanding of the relationship between humans and the environment and to promote sustainable actions. Below are the key aspects that define the nature of environmental education:

*1. Interdisciplinary Approach:* Environmental education draws knowledge from various disciplines, including natural sciences, social sciences, geography, politics, and ethics. This interdisciplinary nature allows for a comprehensive understanding of environmental issues, as these problems are complex and interconnected with multiple dimensions of human life.

• Integration of Disciplines: It combines elements from ecology, biology, chemistry, geography, economics, sociology, and even history to give learners a well-rounded perspective on how human actions impact the natural world.

• Holistic Understanding: By integrating these fields, environmental education helps students understand not only the scientific aspects of the environment but also the social, economic, and political factors that contribute to environmental issues.

*2. Focus on Awareness and Sensitivity:* One of the main objectives of environmental education is to raise awareness and sensitivity to environmental problems. It aims to help individuals and communities recognize the importance of the environment in sustaining life and well-being.

• Awareness of Environmental Challenges: Students learn about key environmental challenges such as climate change, deforestation, pollution, and loss of biodiversity. This awareness is critical for understanding the scale and impact of these issues.

• Sensitivity to Environmental Impacts: Environmental education fosters emotional connections with nature, encouraging individuals to care about the environment and understand how their behaviors affect it.

3. *Emphasis on Sustainability:* A core principle of environmental education is the promotion of sustainability—meeting the needs of the present without compromising the ability of future generations to meet theirs. This focus on sustainability drives home the importance of long-term environmental stewardship.

• Sustainable Practices: Learners are taught how to make choices that reduce environmental impact, such as conserving water, reducing waste, recycling, and using renewable energy sources.

• Balancing Development with Environmental Health: Environmental education emphasizes the need to balance economic and social development with environmental preservation, teaching that human progress should not come at the expense of ecological health.

4. *Development of Problem-Solving Skills:* Environmental education encourages critical thinking and problem-solving skills. Students are taught to analyze environmental problems, consider their root causes, and propose feasible solutions.

• Critical Analysis: Learners are challenged to think critically about the causes of environmental problems and evaluate potential solutions based on scientific evidence, social factors, and ethical considerations.

• Problem-Solving Strategies: Environmental education provides practical tools for solving problems, such as conducting environmental impact assessments, planning for resource management, and developing conservation strategies.

5. *Experiential and Hands-On Learning:* Environmental education often involves direct interaction with the natural environment through fieldwork, outdoor activities, and practical projects. This hands-on approach helps reinforce theoretical knowledge and makes learning more engaging.

• Field Studies: Students may participate in activities like nature walks, biodiversity assessments, and environmental monitoring, which help them observe and understand ecosystems firsthand.

• Community Projects: Environmental education often includes community-based projects, such as planting trees, cleaning rivers, or promoting energy-saving practices. These activities allow learners to apply their knowledge in real-world contexts.

*6. Participation and Action-Oriented:* A key goal of environmental education is to encourage individuals to take active roles in protecting the environment. It seeks to empower people to become responsible citizens who can participate in environmental decision-making and take meaningful action.

• Empowerment: By involving individuals in conservation activities, EE helps foster a sense of responsibility and encourages them to contribute to solving environmental issues.

• Action-Based: Environmental education goes beyond knowledge; it motivates individuals to engage in positive environmental actions, such as advocating for policy changes, participating in environmental campaigns, or adopting sustainable practices in their daily lives.

*7. Value-Based Education:* Environmental education incorporates ethical and moral dimensions, emphasizing the importance of values such as respect for nature, compassion for other species, and responsibility toward future generations.

• Ethical Awareness: It helps learners reflect on their values and beliefs regarding the environment, encouraging behaviors that respect ecosystems, biodiversity, and the intrinsic value of nature.

• Informed Decision-Making: Students are taught to consider the ethical implications of their choices, particularly how those choices impact both local and global ecosystems and communities.

*8. Lifelong Learning Process:* Environmental education is not limited to formal schooling; it is a lifelong learning process. As environmental challenges evolve, individuals of all ages must continually update their knowledge and skills to address new issues.

• Continuous Learning: Environmental education encourages a mindset of curiosity and openness to new information, helping individuals remain informed and engaged with environmental issues throughout their lives.

• Adaptability: As new environmental challenges emerge, such as the effects of climate change or technological advancements, environmental education helps individuals adapt their behaviors and strategies to meet these challenges.

*9. Global and Local Perspective:* Environmental education helps students understand both the global nature of many environmental problems (e.g., climate change, deforestation) and the local solutions that can address them. It encourages a dual perspective that connects global awareness with local action.

• Global Responsibility: Learners are taught that many environmental problems are interconnected on a global scale, requiring international cooperation and collective action to solve.

• Local Engagement: At the same time, environmental education emphasizes the importance of taking local action, such as participating in community clean-ups, conserving local resources, or engaging in policy advocacy at the local level.

*10. Fosters Environmental Stewardship:* Environmental education aims to create environmental stewards—people who are committed to caring for and protecting the environment for future generations. It fosters a sense of ownership and accountability in learners, motivating them to engage in conservation efforts and sustainable practices.

• Stewardship: By promoting a sense of personal responsibility, environmental education encourages individuals to take an active role in conserving natural resources, protecting wildlife, and ensuring the health of ecosystems.

• Long-Term Engagement: Environmental education aims to cultivate a lifelong commitment to environmental protection, rather than viewing it as a one-time effort.

The nature of environmental education is multifaceted and dynamic, focusing on raising awareness, developing critical thinking, and promoting action-oriented learning. It seeks to foster responsible citizens who can make informed decisions and take meaningful actions to protect the environment. By integrating scientific knowledge, ethical values, and practical skills, environmental education empowers individuals to contribute to a more sustainable and just world.

### 6.3.2 Importance of Environmental Education

The importance of environmental education (EE) lies in its ability to raise awareness, develop critical thinking, promote sustainable behaviors, and empower individuals to take meaningful actions toward the protection and preservation of the environment. Environmental education is essential for creating a knowledgeable and responsible society that understands the importance of living in harmony with nature. Key reasons why environmental education is important:

*1. Raises Awareness about Environmental Issues:* Environmental education helps people understand the challenges facing the planet, such as climate change, deforestation, pollution, loss of biodiversity, and resource depletion.

• Knowledge of Environmental Problems: Through environmental education, individuals learn about the causes and consequences of environmental issues at local, national, and global levels. This knowledge helps people recognize the urgency of addressing these problems.

• Informed Decision-Making: By understanding environmental issues, individuals are better equipped to make informed decisions about their personal habits, consumption patterns, and the policies they support.

*2. Promotes Sustainable Development:* Sustainability is a core principle of environmental education. EE teaches people how to live sustainably by balancing economic, social, and environmental needs without compromising the ability of future generations to meet their own needs.

• Fostering Sustainable Practices: Environmental education encourages sustainable habits like reducing waste, conserving water, using renewable energy, and adopting eco-friendly lifestyles. These practices help reduce the human impact on the planet.

• Shaping Future Policies: By teaching individuals about the importance of sustainable development, environmental education helps shape future leaders and policymakers who can implement strategies that ensure long-term environmental health.

*3. Encourages Critical Thinking and Problem-Solving:* Environmental education fosters critical thinking by encouraging learners to analyze complex environmental problems and explore potential solutions.

• Developing Analytical Skills: Learners are trained to critically evaluate environmental issues, considering scientific, social, and ethical perspectives. This helps them develop the skills needed to tackle multifaceted environmental challenges.

• Problem-Solving Capabilities: Environmental education empowers individuals to become active problem solvers. Whether it's through local projects like tree planting or larger-scale advocacy for policy changes, environmental education equips learners with the tools to create positive change.

*4. Empowers Individuals to Take Action:* One of the primary goals of environmental education is to empower individuals to take meaningful action in protecting the environment.

• Active Participation: Environmental education encourages people to engage in environmental conservation activities such as recycling, community clean-up drives, wildlife conservation, and sustainable farming practices.

• Civic Engagement: Environmental education also fosters a sense of responsibility for the planet, motivating people to participate in environmental advocacy, policy-making, and global efforts to mitigate environmental degradation.

5. Fosters Environmental Stewardship Environmental education nurtures a sense of responsibility toward the environment, helping individuals develop a mindset of stewardship.

• Respect for Nature: EE instills values such as respect for all living beings and the recognition of the interconnectedness of life. This helps foster a deep appreciation for the natural world and encourages individuals to act as caretakers of the environment.

• Long-Term Commitment: Environmental stewardship involves a long-term commitment to environmental protection. EE encourages individuals to think beyond their immediate needs and take actions that protect the planet for future generations.

6. *Enhances Quality of Life:* Environmental education contributes to improving the quality of life by promoting practices that lead to healthier environments and communities.

• Healthier Ecosystems: EE emphasizes the importance of protecting ecosystems, which in turn provides cleaner air, water, and food. Healthier ecosystems contribute to improved physical well-being for all living organisms.

• Better Communities: Environmental education also encourages the creation of green spaces, sustainable urban planning, and pollution control, leading to cleaner, more livable communities.

7. *Prepares Individuals for Green Job*s: With the growing demand for sustainability in business, government, and industry, environmental education helps prepare individuals for careers in the green economy.

• Green Job Opportunities: As environmental concerns become more pressing, industries like renewable energy, waste management, and conservation are growing. Environmental education provides the knowledge and skills necessary for individuals to pursue careers in these fields.

• Future-Proofing the Workforce: By focusing on sustainability, environmental education ensures that the workforce is prepared to address emerging environmental challenges and contribute to the transition toward a green economy.

*8. Addresses Global Environmental Challenges :* Environmental education plays a vital role in addressing global environmental challenges by fostering a sense of global citizenship and collective responsibility.

• Global Awareness: EE helps people understand that environmental problems such as climate change, deforestation, and ocean pollution are global in nature. It encourages a mindset that transcends national borders and emphasizes the need for international cooperation.

• Collaborative Solutions: EE promotes the idea that solving environmental problems requires collective action. It encourages people to work together, share knowledge, and support global environmental initiatives.

*9. Builds Resilient Communities:* Environmental education equips individuals and communities with the skills and knowledge needed to adapt to environmental changes and challenges.

• Climate Resilience: EE teaches communities how to adapt to and mitigate the effects of climate change, such as extreme weather events, rising sea levels, and changing agricultural patterns. This helps build more resilient communities that can withstand environmental shocks.

• Sustainable Resource Management: By learning about resource conservation and sustainable agriculture, communities can manage their natural resources more effectively, ensuring long-term food and water security.

*10. Encourages Lifelong Learning :* Environmental education is not limited to formal education settings; it promotes lifelong learning about the environment.

• Continuous Engagement: EE fosters a mindset of curiosity and continuous learning, encouraging individuals to stay informed about environmental issues and take action throughout their lives.

• Adaptation to Change: As environmental issues evolve, individuals need to adapt their understanding and responses. Lifelong environmental education helps people stay aware of new challenges and solutions.

The importance of environmental education cannot be overstated. It plays a critical role in creating informed, responsible, and proactive citizens who are aware of environmental challenges and equipped with the skills to address them. By fostering a culture of sustainability, stewardship, and lifelong learning, environmental education contributes to the well-being of individuals, communities, and the planet. It prepares people for green jobs, builds resilient communities, and empowers individuals to take action at both local and global levels to protect and preserve the environment for future generations.

### 6.4 Programmes of Environmental Education

Environmental education programs across the world, including India, focus on raising awareness, fostering sustainable practices, and promoting environmental stewardship. Several organizations, governments, and institutions run these programs to enhance public knowledge about environmental issues and encourage active participation in solving them. Below are some key fact-based programs from India and around the world:

**Environmental Education Programs in India**

1. National Green Corps (NGC)

• Launched: 2001

• Organized by: Ministry of Environment, Forest and Climate Change (MoEFCC), Government of India

• Target Group: School students

• Description: NGC is a nationwide initiative that creates eco-clubs in schools across India. It involves over 1,00,000 schools and focuses on raising environmental awareness among students through hands-on activities such as tree planting, waste management, and water conservation.

• Impact: Millions of students are engaged in practical environmental activities and projects, fostering a sense of environmental responsibility.

**2. Eco-Club Program (Environment Education Awareness and Training)**

• Launched: 2002

• Organized by: MoEFCC, through State Nodal Agencies

• Target Group: School children

• Description: This program promotes environmental awareness and encourages students to take part in various activities like recycling, waste management, energy conservation, and biodiversity protection. Schools across the country set up eco-clubs to implement sustainable practices.

• Impact: Students become active participants in local environmental projects, gaining knowledge about pressing ecological issues.

**3. Swachh Bharat Mission (Clean India Mission)**

• Launched: 2014

• Organized by: Government of India

• Target Group: Entire population, with a focus on schools and communities

• Description: This national campaign aims to eliminate open defecation and improve waste management in urban and rural areas. Environmental education forms a core component, as students are educated on sanitation, hygiene, and waste disposal through school campaigns and awareness programs.

• Impact: Significant progress has been made in improving sanitation and reducing waste, with a strong emphasis on creating a clean and sustainable environment.

### 4. Environmental Information System (ENVIS)

• Launched: 1982

• Organized by: MoEFCC

• Target Group: General public, researchers, students, policymakers

• Description: ENVIS provides environmental information in a variety of sectors like air pollution, water resources, and biodiversity. It helps in environmental awareness and education by disseminating data and research on key environmental issues.

• Impact: It acts as an information hub, offering valuable insights to the public, environmental researchers, and government agencies for environmental decision-making.

### 5. Centre for Environment Education (CEE)

• Established: 1984

• Organized by: Ministry of Environment and Forests, Government of India

• Target Group: Schools, communities, and professionals

• Description: CEE aims to improve public understanding of environmental challenges and sustainable development. It conducts workshops, campaigns, and projects in schools and communities, focusing on biodiversity conservation, climate change, and water management.

• Impact: CEE has trained thousands of educators and students across India, significantly contributing to environmental awareness and sustainable practices.

### Global Environmental Education Programs

### 1. UNESCO's Education for Sustainable Development (ESD)

• Launched: 2005

• Organized by: United Nations Educational, Scientific and Cultural Organization (UNESCO)

• Target Group: Schools, universities, policymakers, communities worldwide

• Description: ESD integrates environmental education into all levels of education to equip learners with the knowledge and skills needed for sustainable development. It promotes critical thinking, problem-solving, and community action on environmental issues such as climate change, biodiversity, and water conservation.

• Impact: ESD has been implemented in more than 100 countries, enhancing global environmental literacy and encouraging sustainable practices in communities and schools.

**2. The Global Learning and Observations to Benefit the Environment (GLOBE) Program**

• Launched: 1995

• Organized by: NASA, NOAA, and the U.S. Department of State

• Target Group: Schools and educators in over 120 countries

• Description: GLOBE engages students in hands-on science projects and environmental monitoring. Through collaborations with scientists, students collect data on atmosphere, water, soil, and ecosystems, contributing to global environmental research.

• Impact: The program connects students to real-world environmental issues, with over 10 million students contributing to scientific data collection worldwide.

**3. Earthwatch Institute**

• Launched: 1971

• Organized by: Earthwatch

• Target Group: Volunteers, educators, scientists

• Description: Earthwatch focuses on citizen science, where volunteers participate in scientific field research to address environmental challenges like climate change, habitat loss, and ocean health. It emphasizes environmental education through field expeditions.

• Impact: Thousands of volunteers have participated in projects that help gather crucial data on environmental issues while raising awareness and fostering environmental stewardship.

**4. Eco-Schools Program**

• Launched: 1994

• Organized by: Foundation for Environmental Education (FEE)

• Target Group: Schools in 68 countries

• Description: Eco-Schools is an international program that aims to raise students' awareness of sustainability issues. Schools follow a seven-step process to become more sustainable in areas such as waste, water, energy, and biodiversity.

• Impact: The program has reached over 19 million students and 59,000 schools globally, encouraging active participation in environmental projects and sustainable practices.

**5. The World Wide Fund for Nature (WWF) Education Programs**

• Launched: 1961 (WWF established)

• Organized by: WWF International

• Target Group: Schools, communities, policymakers

• Description: WWF runs various environmental education programs to raise awareness about biodiversity conservation, climate action, and wildlife protection. Programs like WWF's "Education for Nature" offer resources and learning materials to schools to promote conservation education.

• Impact: WWF's programs have been implemented in schools and communities across the globe, promoting conservation and sustainable development.

Environmental education programs in India and around the world play a crucial role in addressing the growing environmental challenges of our time. From grassroots initiatives in schools to global campaigns, these programs foster environmental stewardship, raise awareness, and encourage sustainable behaviors. Through hands-on activities, information dissemination, and community involvement, they help create a future where individuals are equipped with the knowledge and skills to protect the planet.

# VII
# Population Education

In a world facing rapid population growth, shrinking resources, and environmental challenges, understanding the dynamics of human populations has become more important than ever. As countries strive to achieve sustainable development, managing population trends and their impact on society is essential for creating a balanced future. This is where population education plays a vital role. It not only raises awareness about demographic changes but also prepares individuals to respond to the challenges posed by these shifts through informed decisions and responsible actions.

## 7.1 Concept & Meaning of Population Education

*Concept of Population Education:*

Population education is an interdisciplinary approach that involves educating individuals about population dynamics and their consequences for society, the economy, and the environment. It emphasizes the importance of understanding how changes in population size, structure, and distribution influence all aspects of human life and development. The core aim of population education is to raise awareness and encourage responsible decision-making regarding population-related issues, such as family planning, migration, urbanization, and resource management.

By understanding population trends, such as *birth rates, death rates, migration patterns, and age structures,* individuals and communities are better equipped to plan for future growth and challenges. Population education thus seeks to provide learners with the skills and knowledge necessary to analyze population data, predict future demographic shifts, and respond to the potential social, environmental, and economic impacts of those changes.

*Meaning of Population Education:*

Population education is an organized effort to teach individuals about the interrelationship between population dynamics and various societal and environmental factors. The meaning of population education extends beyond demographic statistics; it includes the study of the human population's role in shaping economic systems, environmental sustainability, public health, and social structures. It is also concerned with the choices individuals make regarding reproductive health, family size, and consumption patterns, and how those choices collectively influence the population at large.

Population education helps people understand the challenges posed by growing populations—such as resource depletion, environmental stress, and urbanization—while also presenting solutions through family planning, education, and sustainable development practices. It encourages a holistic view of population-related issues, recognizing that human behavior directly influences the well-being of societies and the planet.

Definitions of Population Education:

**1. UNESCO's Definition**: According to UNESCO, population education is "an educational program that provides for a study of population situation in the family, community, nation, and the world, with the purpose of developing rational and responsible attitudes and behavior towards that situation." This definition highlights the idea that population education helps learners understand population issues on various scales, from the local to the global level, while encouraging informed and responsible actions.

**2. National Council of Educational Research and Training (NCERT)**: NCERT defines population education as "the process of helping people understand the nature, causes, and consequences of population growth and its impact on individuals, families, communities, nations, and the world." This definition emphasizes the cause-and-effect relationship of population changes and their widespread implications, underscoring the need for awareness and proactive planning.

**3. Population Reference Bureau (PRB)**: Population education is described as "an approach that integrates the understanding of demographic trends with social, economic, and environmental issues, aiming to equip individuals with the knowledge and skills to address population challenges through sustainable choices and responsible behavior." Each of these definitions stresses that population education is not just about numbers but about understanding the larger context of human existence and how populations interact with finite resources, environmental conditions, and social institutions.

Some important key Areas Covered in Population Education:

• Population Dynamics: Understanding population growth rates, birth and death rates, age distribution, migration patterns, and how they impact economies, ecosystems, and infrastructures.

• Family Planning and Reproductive Health: Learning about the importance of family planning, contraception, and reproductive health in managing population growth and ensuring the well-being of individuals and families.

• Sustainable Development: Promoting sustainable resource use and balanced population growth as a way to protect the environment and ensure that future generations can meet their own needs.

• Social and Economic Impacts: Exploring how population changes affect employment, education, healthcare, housing, and social services.

• Environmental Concerns: Studying the impact of population growth on the environment, including pollution, deforestation, and biodiversity loss.

Population education serves as a crucial educational tool for fostering global citizenship and sustainable practices. It encourages individuals to think critically about population trends and take responsibility for the choices that impact both their personal lives and the world at large.

**Historical Background Of Population Education**

Population education, as a formal educational movement, emerged in response to growing concerns about rapid population growth and its effects on society, the economy, and the environment. Its historical development can be traced through several phases, influenced by both global population trends and the recognition of the need for greater public awareness of population issues.

**1. Early Concerns about Population Growth (18th and 19th Centuries):**

The foundations of population education can be linked to early demographic studies and debates surrounding population growth. Notable among these was the work of Thomas Malthus, an 18th-century British economist, who published his famous essay *"An Essay on the Principle of Population"* in 1798. Malthus argued that unchecked population growth would outpace food production, leading to widespread famine and poverty. This idea sparked debates about the potential consequences of overpopulation, but it wasn't until the 20th century that organized educational efforts on population issues began to take shape.

## 2. Post-World War II Period and the Population Explosion (1940s–1960s):

The post-World War II period marked a dramatic increase in global population growth rates, often referred to as the "population explosion." The advent of modern medicine, improvements in public health, and advances in agricultural productivity (Green Revolution) led to longer life expectancy and a sharp decline in mortality rates, especially in developing countries.

During this time, global concerns over rapid population growth began to mount, as it became clear that unchecked growth could lead to severe social, economic, and environmental problems. International organizations such as the United Nations and its agencies, including UNESCO (United Nations Educational, Scientific and Cultural Organization), began to study population trends and advocate for the inclusion of population-related issues in educational curricula. However, formal population education programs were still in their infancy.

## 3. Emergence of Population Education Programs (1960s–1970s):

The 1960s and 1970s saw the formalization of population education programs, spurred by international conferences and the work of organizations focused on population issues.

• 1960s: The concern over the rapid population growth was formally recognized at the 1965 World Population Conference in Belgrade, where discussions emphasized the need for population control measures and family planning programs. During this period, several countries, particularly in Asia and Latin America, began to explore ways to integrate population issues into their educational systems.

• United Nations and Population Control: The UN began playing an active role in promoting population education as a tool to address global population growth. In 1969, the United Nations Population Fund (UNFPA) was established to assist countries in addressing population issues, including population education, family planning, and reproductive health.

• India as a Pioneer: India was one of the first countries to introduce a national family planning program in the 1950s, and by the 1970s, it also began to incorporate population education into school curricula. This marked the beginning of population education as a formal discipline, focusing on raising awareness about birth control, family size, and the socioeconomic consequences of population growth.

**4. Global Expansion of Population Education (1980s–1990s):**

By the 1980s, population education had gained momentum as a global educational movement. Many countries, especially in Asia, Africa, and Latin America, introduced population education programs in response to the challenges posed by rapid population growth. Governments, non-governmental organizations (NGOs), and international agencies collaborated to develop curricula that included lessons on family planning, demographic trends, resource management, and sustainable development.

• *UNESCO's Role*: UNESCO became a major proponent of population education, helping countries develop population education curricula for schools and teacher training programs. In 1981, UNESCO launched the "Population Education Program" to support the inclusion of population issues in educational institutions worldwide.

• *International Conferences:* The 1984 International Conference on Population in Mexico City and the 1994 International Conference on Population and Development (ICPD) in Cairo were pivotal in shaping the global population education agenda. The ICPD emphasized the importance of integrating population education with broader goals, such as gender equality, reproductive health, and sustainable development. The focus shifted from mere population control to empowering individuals through education to make informed choices about family size and resource use.

**5. Integration with Sustainable Development (2000s–Present):**

In the 21$^{st}$ century, the focus of population education has expanded to address the complex relationships between population growth, resource consumption, and environmental sustainability. With the advent of the Sustainable Development Goals (SDGs), population education is now viewed as a critical tool for achieving sustainable development, particularly in areas such as poverty reduction, gender equality, and environmental conservation.

• Environmental and Social Focus: As concerns about climate change and environmental degradation have grown, population education has increasingly emphasized the need for sustainable practices. This includes teaching about how population dynamics affect ecosystems, resource use, and urban development.

• Family Planning and Reproductive Rights: The rights-based approach to population education now includes an emphasis on reproductive health, family planning, and women's empowerment. Educating individuals, especially women and youth, about their reproductive rights and access to healthcare is seen as a way to promote social equity and control population growth sustainably.

The historical development of population education reflects the growing recognition of population growth as a critical factor in global development. From early concerns about overpopulation to the contemporary focus on sustainability and reproductive rights, population education has evolved to meet the challenges of each era. Today, it is a key part of global efforts to promote responsible decision-making, environmental conservation, and sustainable development.

### 7.1.1 Importance of Population Education

Population education plays a critical role in addressing the complex challenges that arise from population growth, resource management, and sustainable development. By equipping individuals with the knowledge and understanding of demographic trends and their effects, population education fosters informed decision-making, responsible behavior, and long-term planning. Below are several key reasons why population education is important:

**1. Understanding Population Dynamics and Trends:**

Population education helps individuals comprehend basic population concepts such as birth rates, death rates, fertility rates, migration, and population distribution. Understanding these dynamics is crucial for recognizing how population growth impacts various aspects of life, from resource availability to economic development and environmental sustainability. It also enables individuals and policymakers to anticipate future trends and challenges, facilitating better planning and resource allocation.

**2. Addressing Population Growth and Its Consequences:**

One of the primary goals of population education is to raise awareness about the consequences of rapid population growth, such as overpopulation, urban overcrowding, and pressure on natural resources. As populations grow, the demand for food, water, healthcare, education, and housing increases, often leading to resource scarcity and environmental degradation. Population education informs people about these issues and encourages practices that reduce pressure on resources, such as family planning, sustainable agriculture, and responsible consumption.

**3. Promoting Family Planning and Reproductive Health:**

Population education provides essential information about family planning, birth control, and reproductive health, which empowers individuals, particularly women, to make informed choices about their reproductive lives. By promoting awareness of contraception and reproductive health services, population education helps reduce unplanned pregnancies, lower fertility rates, and improve maternal and child health outcomes. It also supports efforts to reduce the spread of sexually transmitted infections (STIs) and promote safe reproductive practices.

### 4. Contributing to Sustainable Development:

As global populations grow, the need for sustainable development becomes more pressing. Population education is directly linked to sustainable development by promoting the responsible use of resources and encouraging practices that protect the environment for future generations. Through education, individuals learn about the importance of balancing population growth with the environment's capacity to support human activities. This understanding fosters the adoption of sustainable lifestyles, reduced waste, and practices like recycling, water conservation, and renewable energy use, all of which are crucial to maintaining ecological balance.

### 5. Enhancing Economic and Social Development:

Population education supports economic development by helping individuals and policymakers understand how population trends influence labor markets, infrastructure needs, and social services. For instance, educating young people about family planning can reduce the number of dependents per household, allowing families to invest more in education and health. In turn, this contributes to the creation of a more educated and healthier workforce, promoting economic growth and poverty reduction. Additionally, by addressing issues like population density and migration, population education can help governments make better decisions regarding urban planning, housing, and transportation.

### 6. Empowering Women and Promoting Gender Equality:

Population education plays a pivotal role in promoting gender equality by empowering women with knowledge about their reproductive rights, family planning, and access to healthcare. When women have control over their reproductive health and are informed about their choices, they are more likely to pursue education and employment, contributing to both their personal development and broader economic growth. Furthermore, reducing fertility rates through family planning allows women to participate more fully in the workforce, further promoting gender equality and societal progress.

**7. Reducing Poverty and Improving Quality of Life:**

There is a strong link between rapid population growth, poverty, and quality of life. Overpopulated areas often experience higher levels of poverty, unemployment, and poor living conditions. Population education can help mitigate these issues by teaching people about the benefits of smaller family sizes, responsible parenting, and the efficient use of resources. This, in turn, leads to better educational opportunities, improved health outcomes, and greater economic stability for individuals and families, ultimately contributing to a higher quality of life.

**8. Addressing Environmental Issues:**

Population education highlights the impact of human activities on the environment, particularly the strain placed on natural resources due to overpopulation. It educates individuals about the importance of protecting ecosystems, biodiversity, and the natural environment from degradation caused by deforestation, pollution, and climate change. By understanding the link between population growth and environmental sustainability, individuals are more likely to adopt environmentally friendly practices such as reducing carbon footprints, conserving water and energy, and supporting reforestation efforts.

**9. Promoting Global Awareness and Cooperation:**

Population issues are not confined to individual countries; they are global in nature, affecting the entire world. Population education fosters global awareness by helping individuals understand how population trends in one region can have far-reaching impacts on global economics, migration patterns, and environmental sustainability. It also encourages international cooperation in addressing population challenges, as countries must work together to find solutions for shared concerns like climate change, resource depletion, and public health crises.

**10. Preparing for Demographic Shifts:**

Population education prepares societies for significant demographic shifts, such as aging populations, declining birth rates, or migration surges. These changes can strain healthcare systems, pension schemes, and social services if not properly planned for. Population education enables individuals and governments to anticipate and adapt to these shifts, ensuring that policies and infrastructure are in place to support aging populations, integrate immigrants, and sustain economic growth.

**11. Improving Health Outcomes:**

By educating people about the importance of reproductive health, family planning, and disease prevention, population education leads to better health outcomes for both individuals and communities. Knowledge of maternal health, prenatal care, and childhood vaccinations, for example, reduces maternal and infant mortality rates. Moreover, awareness of sexually transmitted infections (STIs) and preventive measures helps curb the spread of diseases, contributing to healthier populations overall.

Population education is essential for individuals, communities, and nations to address the challenges posed by population growth, resource consumption, and environmental sustainability. It empowers people with the knowledge and skills necessary to make informed decisions about family planning, resource use, and social development. By fostering responsible behavior and promoting sustainable practices, population education contributes to a more equitable and sustainable future for all. It is a crucial tool in creating a balanced relationship between human populations and the ecosystems that support them.

### 7.1.2 Objectives Of Population Education

The objectives of population education are designed to create awareness, understanding, and responsible behavior among individuals regarding the dynamics of population growth, its effects on society, and the sustainable management of resources. Population education aims to equip learners with the necessary knowledge, attitudes, and skills to make informed decisions about population-related issues. Below are the key objectives of population education, elaborated in detail:

**A) To Create Awareness of Population Issues:** One of the primary objectives of population education is to raise awareness about global and local population issues. These include overpopulation, aging populations, migration, urbanization, and declining fertility rates. By understanding these issues, individuals become more conscious of the impact population trends have on economic development, social structures, and environmental sustainability. Population education encourages individuals to engage with and contribute to discussions and policies related to population management.

**B) To Foster Understanding of Population Dynamics:** Population education seeks to deepen the understanding of population dynamics, which include factors such as birth rates, death rates, fertility rates, migration patterns, and demographic transitions. These elements are critical in analyzing how populations grow or decline, how they age, and how they move across regions. A clear understanding of these dynamics helps learners grasp the complexity of population trends and how they influence social, economic, and environmental changes.

**C) To Promote Knowledge of Reproductive Health and Family Planning:** A central goal of population education is to provide information about reproductive health, including the principles of family planning, contraception, and responsible parenthood. Educating individuals—especially adolescents and young adults—about sexual and reproductive health empowers them to make informed decisions regarding family size, childbearing, and birth spacing. This knowledge leads to better health outcomes, reduces the incidence of unintended pregnancies, and contributes to the overall well-being of families.

**D) To Encourage Responsible Behavior Regarding Population Growth:** Population education aims to promote responsible attitudes and behavior toward population growth and resource management. This includes teaching individuals about the consequences of rapid population growth, such as increased demand for housing, food, healthcare, and other services. By fostering a sense of responsibility, population education encourages individuals to make thoughtful decisions about family size, consumption, and the use of natural resources to avoid putting undue pressure on the environment and society.

**E) To Highlight the Link Between Population Growth and Resource Management:** Population education emphasizes the relationship between population growth and the consumption of natural resources such as water, energy, food, and land. Rapid population growth can lead to resource depletion, environmental degradation, and increased competition for scarce resources. The objective here is to create awareness about the importance of sustainable resource management and the need for careful planning to balance population growth with the availability of natural resources.

**F) To Promote Gender Equality and Women's Empowerment:** Another objective of population education is to highlight the importance of gender equality and the empowerment of women in managing population growth. By educating women about their reproductive rights, access to healthcare, and family planning options, population education helps women make informed decisions regarding childbearing. This, in turn, supports broader efforts to reduce poverty, improve maternal and child health, and foster gender equality, as empowered women tend to have smaller, healthier families and greater opportunities for education and employment.

**G) To Support Sustainable Development:** Population education is closely linked to the goal of sustainable development. It teaches individuals the importance of balancing population growth with the carrying capacity of the environment. By fostering sustainable practices such as conservation, recycling, and responsible consumption, population education helps ensure that future generations will have access to the resources they need for a decent quality of life. This objective is aligned with global efforts to achieve the Sustainable Development Goals (SDGs), particularly those related to poverty reduction, environmental protection, and equitable economic growth.

**H) To Develop Critical Thinking and Problem-Solving Skills:** Population education encourages learners to think critically about the challenges posed by population growth and how to address them effectively. It promotes the development of problem-solving skills, enabling individuals to analyze population trends, assess their impact on society and the environment, and propose solutions to population-related challenges. This objective helps learners develop the capacity to engage with complex, real-world problems and take active roles in addressing issues such as urbanization, food security, and resource management.

**I) To Raise Awareness About the Consequences of Overpopulation:** One of the primary concerns of population education is overpopulation and its far-reaching consequences. Overpopulation can lead to numerous challenges, including environmental degradation, unemployment, poverty, insufficient housing, and poor public health. By highlighting these potential outcomes, population education aims to encourage individuals and governments to adopt policies that help mitigate the negative impacts of overpopulation, such as through family planning programs, education, and sustainable urban development.

**J) To Prepare for Demographic Changes:** Population education prepares individuals and societies for major demographic changes, such as an aging population, migration, or declining birth rates. These shifts can present challenges for governments in terms of healthcare, pensions, and social services. Population education equips individuals with the tools needed to understand and respond to these demographic shifts, ensuring that they can plan for the future and adapt to changes in population structure.

**K) To Encourage Global Cooperation and Awareness:** Population issues are global in nature, and population education encourages individuals to view population trends from a global perspective. The objective is to foster a sense of global citizenship by making people aware that population dynamics in one part of the world can have ripple effects across borders. For example, population pressure in one region may lead to migration, while overconsumption in wealthy nations can contribute to resource depletion and environmental damage worldwide. Population education thus promotes international cooperation in addressing global challenges such as climate change, resource management, and poverty alleviation.

**L) To Improve Quality of Life Ultimately:** The overarching objective of population education is to improve the quality of life for individuals, families, and communities. By teaching people about family planning, sustainable living, and responsible resource management, population education contributes to a healthier, more balanced society where people can live in harmony with the environment. This objective is aimed at reducing poverty, improving health outcomes, and ensuring that future generations can enjoy a higher standard of living.

The objectives of population education are multi-faceted, addressing a wide range of population-related issues, from reproductive health to sustainable development. By raising awareness, fostering critical thinking, and promoting responsible behavior, population education helps individuals and societies navigate the challenges of population growth, resource management, and environmental conservation. Its ultimate goal is to equip people with the knowledge and skills necessary to contribute to a sustainable and equitable future for all.

### 7.2 Population Explosion

**Concept and Meaning of Population Explosion:**

Population explosion refers to a rapid and sudden increase in the size of a population, particularly within a short period. This phenomenon is characterized by an excessively high birth rate, low mortality rate, and overall growth in the number of people within a particular region or globally. Population explosion typically occurs when the birth rate significantly exceeds the death rate, leading to a substantial increase in the number of people in a relatively short amount of time.

Population explosion is often linked to advances in healthcare, improved living conditions, and a reduction in mortality rates due to medical innovations and better access to nutrition and hygiene. While population growth is natural, when it reaches extreme levels without corresponding growth in resources and infrastructure, it can create severe socio-economic and environmental challenges.

Characteristics of Population Explosion:

• High Birth Rate: A sustained period of high fertility, resulting in large numbers of births.

• Low Death Rate: Advances in medicine, sanitation, and food security reduce mortality rates, particularly in infant and maternal health.

• Rapid Growth in Short Time: Population growth that outpaces the available resources, infrastructure, and services needed to support the growing population.

• Concentration in Certain Regions: Population explosion often occurs more dramatically in developing nations where birth control measures may be limited and healthcare improvements lead to sudden decreases in mortality.

**Definitions of Population Explosion:**

1. Dictionary Definition: *"Population explosion is the rapid and excessive increase in population, particularly in areas with limited resources, leading to challenges such as overcrowding, unemployment, and environmental degradation."*

2. According to the United Nations (UN): *"A population explosion refers to the rapid increase in the number of individuals in a population, which can lead to significant pressures on social and environmental systems if the growth is not matched by resources or effective planning."*

3. Sociological Definition: *"Population explosion is the unregulated and exponential increase in population size that results from high birth rates and declining death rates, creating imbalances in social, economic, and environmental spheres."*

4. Biological Definition: *"In biological terms, population explosion refers to a sudden and large increase in the number of individuals in a particular species, particularly in response to favorable environmental conditions".*

**7.2.1 Causes of Population Explosion**

Population explosion occurs when the birth rate exceeds the death rate, leading to a rapid increase in the number of individuals in a population. Several factors contribute to this phenomenon, particularly in developing countries where improvements in healthcare and living conditions often coexist with high fertility rates. Below are the primary causes of population explosion:

**i) Decline in Death Rates (Increased Life Expectancy):** One of the major factors behind population explosion is a significant decline in death rates due to advancements in medical science and healthcare. Improved access to medical facilities, vaccinations, better sanitation, and nutrition have led to lower infant mortality rates and longer life expectancy. Common causes of death such as infectious diseases, malnutrition, and poor maternal health, which used to claim many lives, are now better managed through medical interventions, leading to more people living longer lives.

**ii) High Birth Rates (Fertility Rates):** In many regions, especially in developing countries, birth rates remain high due to cultural, social, and economic factors. High fertility rates are often seen in societies where large families are valued for various reasons, such as the economic benefits of having more hands for labor (especially in agricultural economies) or social norms that encourage having many children. The lack of widespread family planning and contraceptive use contributes to consistently high fertility rates, further accelerating population growth.

**iii) Lack of Family Planning and Contraceptive Use:** A key contributor to population explosion is the limited use or availability of family planning methods. In many parts of the world, access to contraception is restricted due to lack of education, cultural taboos, religious beliefs, or economic barriers. Additionally, in areas where health services are underdeveloped, there may be a lack of adequate information on birth control methods, leading to unintended pregnancies and large families. This absence of family planning contributes to an uncontrolled rise in the population.

**iv) Cultural and Religious Factors:** Cultural and religious beliefs can play a significant role in population growth. In many traditional societies, large families are seen as a sign of wealth and social status. Cultural norms may encourage having many children, while some religious beliefs promote the idea of procreation as a moral or spiritual duty. In such contexts, the use of contraceptives or family planning methods may be discouraged, resulting in higher birth rates and faster population growth.

**v) Early Marriage and Childbearing:** In societies where child marriage is prevalent, women often begin having children at a younger age, leading to longer reproductive periods and higher fertility rates over their lifetimes. Early marriages also contribute to the social expectation of having more children, as women tend to have multiple pregnancies when married at a younger age. This cultural practice is common in some developing countries, where girls marry in their teenage years, resulting in larger families over time.

**vi) Poverty and Economic Factors:** In many developing regions, poverty contributes to high fertility rates, as children are often viewed as economic assets. In agrarian societies, for example, children are expected to contribute to farm labor and family income. As a result, families may choose to have more children to ensure a larger workforce. Additionally, in regions with limited social security systems, parents may have many children as a form of "insurance" for old age, with the expectation that their children will take care of them later in life.

**vii) Improved Agricultural Production:** Advancements in agricultural technology and food production have helped sustain larger populations by reducing food scarcity. The Green Revolution, for instance, introduced high-yield crop varieties, improved irrigation techniques, and the use of fertilizers and pesticides, which significantly boosted food production in countries with growing populations. With the availability of more food, populations that previously faced hunger or famine are able to sustain higher growth rates, contributing to the population explosion.

**viii) Immigration:** Population explosion can also occur due to immigration, particularly when there is a significant influx of people into a region or country with better living conditions and economic opportunities. While this may not directly affect global population numbers, the arrival of large numbers of immigrants in certain areas can lead to localized population booms. Countries with higher levels of immigration may experience sudden increases in their population, putting pressure on local resources and services.

**ix) Lack of Education, Particularly Among Women:** Education, particularly for women, is one of the most important factors in controlling population growth. In regions where women have limited access to education, fertility rates tend to be higher. Educated women are more likely to delay marriage, seek employment, and have fewer children. In contrast, women with little or no education often marry at younger ages and have more children. Population education and awareness about family planning are crucial in addressing this issue, but in many areas, the lack of education continues to drive population growth.

**x) Medical Advancements in Fertility Treatments:** Advances in fertility treatments and reproductive technology, such as in-vitro fertilization (IVF), have also contributed to population growth, especially in regions with declining fertility rates. While this is not a primary cause in most developing countries, it does contribute to population growth in regions where fertility challenges are addressed through medical intervention, enabling more individuals and couples to have children.

**xi) Urbanization and Reduced Infant Mortality:** Urbanization has led to better access to healthcare, improved hygiene, and better living standards, which contribute to lower infant mortality rates. In the past, high infant mortality rates often balanced out high birth rates, but with better healthcare, more children are surviving to adulthood, resulting in faster population growth. Urban areas tend to have more advanced medical facilities that can reduce both infant and maternal deaths, encouraging larger populations to form in cities and urbanized region.

The population explosion is a multifaceted phenomenon driven by a combination of medical, cultural, economic, and social factors. A decline in death rates, high fertility rates, lack of family planning, poverty, early marriages, and cultural values that support large families are some of the main drivers. While advances in healthcare and agriculture have made it possible to sustain larger populations, the rapid growth has placed immense pressure on natural resources, infrastructure, and social services. Addressing the root causes of population explosion requires comprehensive policies that include education, family planning services, and sustainable development strategies.

## 7.3 Population Growth

Population growth refers to the increase in the number of people in a particular area over a specific period. It is a dynamic process driven by the interplay of birth rates, death rates, and migration. Population growth has significant implications for society, the economy, the environment, and overall human development. While population growth can contribute to economic progress by providing a larger workforce, unchecked growth can strain resources, infrastructure, and the environment, leading to challenges such as poverty, unemployment, and ecological degradation.

### Concept of Population Growth

At its core, population growth is the change in population size over time. This growth can either be positive (population increase) or negative (population decline). When birth rates exceed death rates, the population increases, leading to positive growth. Conversely, when death rates outpace birth rates or when large numbers of people emigrate, the population decreases, leading to negative growth.

Population growth can be natural or influenced by migration:

• Natural Growth: This is the increase in population due to more births and fewer deaths.

• Growth through Migration: This occurs when the number of immigrants exceeds the number of emigrants, leading to a net population increase in a specific region.

**Factors Influencing Population Growth**

Population growth is influenced by several key factors, which are intertwined with social, economic, cultural, and environmental conditions. These factors include:

A. *Birth Rates (Fertility)* Birth rate, also known as the fertility rate, refers to the number of live births in a population over a specific period. High birth rates typically contribute to rapid population growth, especially in developing countries where access to family planning services may be limited. Fertility rates are influenced by several factors, including:

• Cultural and religious beliefs: Societies that value large families or view children as a form of social security tend to have higher birth rates.

• Economic factors: In many agricultural communities, children are seen as contributors to the family's labor force, leading to higher fertility rates.

• Education and employment: Lower levels of education, particularly among women, are associated with higher birth rates, while increased access to education and employment opportunities tend to reduce fertility rates.

B. *Death Rates (Mortality)* The death rate, or mortality rate, measures the number of deaths in a population over a specific period. A significant decline in death rates is one of the main factors contributing to population growth, especially in countries where medical advancements, better sanitation, and improved living standards have reduced mortality. Lower death rates are driven by:

• Advances in healthcare: Improvements in medical technology, vaccinations, and the availability of healthcare have reduced death rates, especially in younger populations.

• Sanitation and nutrition: Improved access to clean water, better nutrition, and enhanced hygiene practices contribute to longer life expectancies and lower mortality rates.

C. *Migration* is the movement of people from one region to another, either within a country or across international borders. Migration can significantly affect population growth, especially in urban areas or countries experiencing high levels of immigration. Migration patterns are influenced by factors such as:

• Economic opportunities: People move to areas with better job prospects, leading to population increases in those regions.

• Conflict and displacement: Wars, political instability, and natural disasters can drive people from their homes, leading to population increases in safe regions and declines in areas of conflict.

*D. Government policies* can have a direct impact on population growth. Some governments may encourage population growth by offering incentives for larger families, while others may implement population control measures to curb rapid growth.

For example:

• Pro-natalist policies: Countries with aging populations or labor shortages may introduce incentives like tax benefits, parental leave, and child allowances to encourage families to have more children.

• Anti-natalist policies: In contrast, some countries, like China with its one-child policy (now relaxed), have implemented policies to limit population growth to avoid overpopulation and strain on resources.

**Stages of Population Growth**

Population growth follows a general pattern known as the Demographic Transition Model (DTM), which explains the changes in birth and death rates as a country develops from a pre-industrial to an industrialized economic system. There are typically four to five stages:

*Stage 1: High Stationary*

• High birth and death rates: In this stage, both birth rates and death rates are high, resulting in a stable and low population. This is typical of pre-industrial societies where disease, famine, and limited medical care lead to high mortality rates.

• Slow or stagnant growth: Due to high mortality, population growth is slow or stagnant.

*Stage 2: Early Expanding*

• High birth rate and falling death rate: As societies begin to industrialize, improvements in healthcare, nutrition, and sanitation reduce death rates, while birth rates remain high.

• Rapid population growth: This stage sees a rapid population increase as more people survive childhood and live longer.

*Stage 3: Late Expanding*

• Declining birth rates and low death rates: As economic and social conditions improve, birth rates begin to fall due to increased urbanization, access to education, and family planning services. Death rates remain low.

• Slowing population growth: Population growth slows as the gap between birth and death rates narrows.

*Stage 4: Low Stationary*

• Low birth and death rates: In developed countries, both birth rates and death rates are low, leading to a stable or slowly growing population.

• Zero or negative growth: At this stage, population growth may stabilize or even decline if birth rates drop below replacement levels (the number of births needed to maintain population size).

*Stage 5: Declining*

• Very low birth rates: In some developed countries, birth rates may fall below death rates, leading to a decline in the population.

• Aging population: As life expectancy increases and birth rates fall, these societies experience an aging population, which can present challenges for healthcare, pensions, and labor markets.

## Consequences of Population Growth

Population growth has wide-ranging consequences, both positive and negative. The impact of population growth varies depending on whether a country has the resources and infrastructure to support its growing population.

*Positive Consequences:*

• Economic Growth: A larger population can contribute to economic growth by providing a larger workforce, more consumers, and increased demand for goods and services.

• Innovation and Development: Population growth can drive innovation as societies develop new technologies and systems to accommodate the needs of a larger population.

*Negative Consequences:*

• Resource Scarcity: Rapid population growth can lead to overconsumption of natural resources, such as water, food, and energy, leading to scarcity and higher prices.

• Environmental Degradation: Overpopulation contributes to deforestation, loss of biodiversity, pollution, and climate change due to the increased consumption of resources and higher levels of waste production.

• Unemployment and Poverty: When population growth outpaces job creation, it can lead to high levels of unemployment and poverty, particularly in developing countries.

• Pressure on Infrastructure: Rapid population growth can strain infrastructure such as housing, healthcare, education, and transportation systems, leading to overcrowding and poor living conditions.

**Managing Population Growth**

Population growth must be managed to ensure sustainable development. Governments, NGOs, and international organizations often focus on measures such as:

• Family Planning Programs: Educating people about birth control methods and providing access to contraceptives can help reduce fertility rates and control population growth.

• Education and Empowerment of Women: Providing education and employment opportunities for women tends to lower birth rates, as educated women are more likely to delay marriage and childbearing and have fewer children.

• Sustainable Development Policies: Governments can promote policies that balance population growth with environmental conservation and resource management.

Population growth is a complex phenomenon influenced by a variety of factors, including birth rates, death rates, migration, and government policies. While it can drive economic development and innovation, uncontrolled population growth poses significant challenges, including resource depletion, environmental degradation, and social inequality. Managing population growth through education, healthcare, and sustainable development policies is essential for creating a balanced and prosperous future for all.

### 7.3.1 Problems of Unemployment

**Concept of Unemployment**

*Unemployment* refers to the condition where individuals who are willing and able to work are unable to find suitable employment. It is a key economic indicator that reflects the health of a country's economy. Unemployment occurs when there is a mismatch between the number of people seeking work and the number of jobs available in the market. It can be caused by various factors, including economic downturns, technological advancements, and structural changes in industries.

Unemployment is generally measured as a percentage of the labor force that is actively seeking work but is not employed. The unemployment rate is a critical measure used by governments and economists to assess economic performance and to design policies aimed at reducing unemployment.

Types of Unemployment that helps in understanding the elaborated concept of Unemployment

*1. Frictional Unemployment:* This type of unemployment occurs when individuals are temporarily unemployed while transitioning between jobs. It is a natural form of unemployment that results from the time it takes for people to find a job that matches their skills and preferences. For example, recent graduates or people who voluntarily leave one job to find another may experience frictional unemployment.

*2. Structural Unemployment:* Structural unemployment occurs when there is a mismatch between the skills of the workforce and the jobs available in the economy. This often happens due to technological changes, shifts in industries, or changes in consumer demand. For instance, if a particular industry declines (e.g., manufacturing) while another grows (e.g., information technology), workers may become structurally unemployed if their skills are no longer in demand.

*3. Cyclical Unemployment:* Cyclical unemployment is related to the overall health of the economy and occurs during periods of economic downturns or recessions. When there is a decline in demand for goods and services, businesses may cut back on production, leading to layoffs and a rise in unemployment. Cyclical unemployment decreases during periods of economic growth and increases during periods of recession.

*4. Seasonal Unemployment:* This type of unemployment occurs in industries that operate seasonally, such as agriculture, tourism, or construction. Workers in these industries may experience periods of unemployment during the off-season when demand for their labor is low.

*5. Underemployment:* While not a traditional form of unemployment, underemployment refers to individuals who are employed but working in jobs that are below their skill level or only part-time when they would prefer full-time employment. This can happen when there is a lack of full-time opportunities or when highly skilled workers are forced to take low-skilled jobs due to economic conditions. Problems of Unemployment Unemployment has far-reaching consequences, not only for the individuals affected but also for society and the economy as a whole.

**Problems :**

Some of the major problems caused by unemployment include:

**1. Economic Problems**

• Loss of Income: Unemployment leads to a loss of income for individuals, which can result in reduced living standards. Without a steady income, people are unable to meet their basic needs such as food, shelter, healthcare, and education, leading to increased poverty levels.

• Reduced Economic Growth: High levels of unemployment can slow down economic growth. When a large portion of the population is unemployed, there is less consumer spending, which can reduce demand for goods and services. This, in turn, leads to lower production levels and fewer investments by businesses, creating a cycle of economic stagnation.

• Increased Government Expenditure: Governments often have to spend more on social welfare programs, such as unemployment benefits, housing assistance, and healthcare for unemployed individuals. This places a strain on public finances and can lead to budget deficits, requiring either higher taxes or reduced spending in other areas such as infrastructure or education.

• Wasted Human Resources: Unemployment results in the underutilization of human resources. Skilled individuals who are unemployed for extended periods may lose their skills or fail to keep up with new developments in their field, making it harder for them to re-enter the workforce in the future.

## 2. Social Problems

• Increased Poverty: Unemployment is a direct cause of poverty, especially when people are unable to secure employment for long periods. Families affected by unemployment may struggle to afford basic necessities, leading to increased reliance on government support and charitable organizations.

• Social Exclusion: Prolonged unemployment can lead to social exclusion, where individuals feel disconnected from society due to their inability to participate in work or social activities. This can create a sense of isolation and marginalization, particularly among young people, the elderly, or those from disadvantaged backgrounds.

• Crime and Social Unrest: High unemployment rates are often linked to increased crime and social unrest. When people are unable to find legitimate ways to earn a living, they may turn to illegal activities, such as theft or drug dealing, to survive. In addition, frustration and hopelessness caused by unemployment can lead to protests, strikes, and other forms of social unrest.

• Mental Health Issues: Unemployment can have a significant impact on an individual's mental health. The stress of being unemployed, coupled with financial insecurity, can lead to anxiety, depression, and other psychological problems. Long-term unemployment can erode self-esteem and create feelings of worthlessness, exacerbating mental health issues.

## 3. Political Problems

• Political Instability: High levels of unemployment can create political instability, as discontented citizens may lose confidence in the government's ability to manage the economy and provide for their needs. This can lead to protests, strikes, or even changes in government leadership as voters demand policies that address unemployment.

• Policy Challenges: Addressing unemployment often requires governments to implement economic and social policies that promote job creation, such as investing in infrastructure, providing job training programs, or offering tax incentives to businesses. However, finding the right balance between stimulating employment and managing public finances can be a major challenge, particularly during times of economic downturn.

### 4. Economic Inequality

• Widening Income Gap: Unemployment often exacerbates economic inequality, as those who are unemployed or underemployed have less access to resources and opportunities compared to those who are employed. This creates a growing divide between the rich and the poor, leading to greater social and economic disparities.

• Generational Poverty: Unemployment, particularly long-term unemployment, can create a cycle of poverty that is passed down through generations. Families affected by unemployment may not be able to afford education for their children, limiting future opportunities for upward mobility and perpetuating economic disadvantage.

Unemployment is a significant social and economic issue that affects individuals, communities, and entire economies. While natural forms of unemployment, such as frictional unemployment, are part of a healthy labor market, high levels of structural or cyclical unemployment can lead to widespread economic and social problems. Addressing unemployment requires a multi-faceted approach, including job creation, education and skills training, social welfare programs, and economic policies that stimulate growth. Governments, businesses, and society as a whole must work together to mitigate the effects of unemployment and create a more inclusive and stable labor market.

# VIII
# Inclusive Education

*"The greatest sign of success for a teacher is to be able to say, 'The children are now working as if I did not exist'."* - **Dr. Maria Montessori**

Equal opportunity in education is a fundamental principle that asserts every individual, regardless of their background, abilities, or socio-economic status, should have access to quality educational resources and experiences. This concept encompasses various dimensions, including inclusivity for students with disabilities, equitable funding for schools in underprivileged areas, and the elimination of discriminatory practices that hinder access to learning. By creating an environment where all students can thrive, equal opportunity in education not only enhances individual potential but also strengthens society as a whole. It promotes diversity, encourages collaboration, and cultivates a culture of empathy and respect. Ultimately, ensuring equal educational opportunities is essential for breaking the cycle of poverty, reducing inequality, and preparing all individuals to contribute positively to their communities and the workforce.

## 8.1 Meaning of Inclusive Education

Inclusive education is a comprehensive approach that ensures all students, regardless of their diverse backgrounds, abilities, or disabilities, have the opportunity to participate fully in the educational process. It seeks to create a learning environment that values diversity, promotes equal access to education, and accommodates the unique needs of each learner.

### Concept of Inclusive Education

*Holistic Approach:* Inclusive education goes beyond simply placing students with disabilities in regular classrooms. It involves adapting teaching methods, curricula, and school environments to accommodate the diverse needs of all students. The goal is to foster an inclusive culture that respects and values differences.

*Equity and Access:* The foundation of inclusive education is the belief that all students should have equal access to quality education. This means removing barriers—whether physical, social, or instructional—that prevent students from fully participating in the learning experience.

*Collaborative Learning:* Inclusive education promotes collaboration among teachers, specialists, and families to support students' individual needs. This often involves developing individualized education plans (IEPs) and using differentiated instruction to cater to varied learning styles and abilities.

*Social Inclusion:* Beyond academic success, inclusive education aims to foster social interactions and relationships among students of all abilities, encouraging empathy, understanding, and cooperation.

**Definitions of Inclusive Education**

*1. UNESCO:* According to UNESCO, inclusive education is *"a process of addressing and responding to the diversity of needs of all learners through increasing participation in learning, cultures, and communities, and reducing exclusion within and from education."*

*2. United Nations Convention on the Rights of Persons with Disabilities (CRPD):* This document emphasizes the right to inclusive education for all individuals with disabilities, stating that *"persons with disabilities should be able to access inclusive, quality, and free primary and secondary education on an equal basis with others."*

*3. The Salamanca Statement (1994):* This UNESCO document states that *"schools should accommodate all children regardless of their physical, intellectual, social, emotional, linguistic, or other conditions."*

It highlights the need for a comprehensive approach to inclusive education, promoting the importance of adapting schools to the diverse needs of students.

*4. The Inclusive Schools Network:* This organization defines inclusive education as *"a philosophy of education that promotes the full participation of all students in the learning environment. It embraces diversity and recognizes that each student has unique strengths and challenges."*

*5. The World Bank:* The World Bank describes inclusive education as *"a system that allows all children to learn together, regardless of their differences in ability, background, or circumstances, ensuring that no child is left behind."*

Inclusive education is a dynamic and evolving concept aimed at ensuring that all students receive equitable access to quality education. By embracing diversity and fostering an inclusive culture, educational institutions can create environments where every learner can thrive academically and socially. Definitions from various international organizations underscore the global commitment to promoting inclusive practices in education, making it an essential aspect of contemporary educational policy and practice.

**Definitions by different Educationists**

"The child is both a hope and a promise for mankind. Education should be directed to the cultivation of the child's inherent potential, providing an inclusive environment that respects the individuality of each child." *-Dr. Maria Montessori*

"Inclusive education is about recognizing and valuing diversity in intelligence and ability. It is an approach that ensures all students, regardless of their learning differences, can thrive in a shared learning environment." *-Dr. Howard Gardner*

"Inclusive education is about addressing the diversity of students in the classroom by creating a culture of belonging where everyone feels valued and supported to learn." *-Dr. Lani Florian*

"Inclusive education is a philosophy that advocates for the right of every student to learn alongside their peers, with the necessary support and adaptations in place to ensure their success." *-Dr. Richard A. Villa*

"Inclusive education is about providing all children with the opportunity to participate fully in their education, regardless of their individual needs or circumstances."

"Inclusive education means that all students, regardless of their abilities or disabilities, should learn together in the same classroom, supported by appropriate resources and teaching strategies." *-Dr. Peter Mittler*

"Inclusive education is about creating a school community where all students can learn together, where differences are embraced and celebrated, and where every student is given the opportunity to succeed." *- Dr. Thomas Hehir*

These definitions emphasize that inclusive education is a philosophy rooted in the belief that all students, regardless of their backgrounds or abilities, should have the right to learn together in an equitable and supportive environment. The focus on individuality, diversity, and community reflects a commitment to fostering educational systems that cater to the needs of every learner.

### 8.1.1 Objectives of Inclusive Education

The objectives of inclusive education are aimed at creating an equitable, diverse, and supportive learning environment where all students, regardless of their backgrounds, abilities, or needs, have the opportunity to succeed. Below is a detailed exploration of these objectives:

**1. Ensuring Equal Access to Quality Education**

• Objective: To provide all students, including those with disabilities, socio-economic disadvantages, or from minority groups, with the opportunity to access quality education in the same classroom.

• Explanation: Inclusive education seeks to eliminate barriers to access, ensuring that no child is excluded from mainstream education based on their differences. This objective is centered on the principle that every child deserves a fair chance to participate in learning, and that schools should be equipped to accommodate diverse needs.

**2. Promoting Equity and Reducing Discrimination**

• Objective: To promote equity by reducing social, educational, and economic disparities and eliminating discrimination in the learning environment.

• Explanation: Inclusive education aims to foster a culture of equality, where differences in ability, ethnicity, gender, or socioeconomic status are respected and valued. This objective ensures that education systems do not privilege one group over another and that students feel safe and respected in their learning environment. It also involves challenging negative attitudes, stigmas, and stereotypes that may arise due to diversity.

**3. Fostering a Sense of Belonging**

• Objective: To ensure that all students feel accepted, valued, and included within the school community, promoting a sense of belonging.

• Explanation: Inclusion is not only about physical placement in a classroom but also about emotional and social integration. A key objective of inclusive education is to create an environment where every student feels like an integral part of the school community, fostering confidence and self-worth. This sense of belonging is crucial for developing positive relationships among students and creating a collaborative and respectful learning environment.

**4. Enhancing Learning Outcomes for All Students**

• Objective: To improve academic and social outcomes for all students by providing appropriate support and resources to meet diverse learning needs.

• Explanation: Inclusive education focuses on improving educational outcomes for all learners, not just those with special needs. This is achieved through differentiated instruction, the use of individualized education plans (IEPs), and employing various teaching strategies that cater to different learning styles. The objective is to ensure that each student can reach their full potential, whether they are academically advanced or need additional support.

### 5. Developing Social and Emotional Skills

• Objective: To promote the development of social and emotional skills, such as empathy, teamwork, and conflict resolution, by encouraging interaction between students of diverse abilities and backgrounds.

• Explanation: Inclusive classrooms provide opportunities for students to learn social skills by interacting with peers who have different abilities and experiences. These interactions foster empathy, compassion, and mutual respect, preparing students for real-world social situations. By promoting collaboration and understanding, inclusive education helps to develop emotionally intelligent, well-rounded individuals.

### 6. Supporting Teacher Development and Capacity Building

• Objective: To enhance the professional development of teachers, enabling them to effectively meet the diverse needs of students in an inclusive setting.

• Explanation: Teachers play a critical role in the success of inclusive education. This objective focuses on equipping educators with the knowledge, skills, and resources to handle diverse classrooms. It involves continuous training on inclusive teaching strategies, behavior management, and the use of assistive technologies to accommodate students with special needs. Additionally, fostering a collaborative culture among teachers, specialists, and families is essential to ensure that students receive the support they need.

### 7. Creating an Inclusive Curriculum

• Objective: To develop a curriculum that is flexible and accessible, catering to the diverse learning needs, interests, and abilities of all students.

• Explanation:An inclusive curriculum is designed to be adaptable, allowing teachers to modify lessons and materials to suit different learning styles and abilities. This objective ensures that all students can engage with the curriculum meaningfully, whether through visual aids, hands-on activities, or technology-assisted learning. The curriculum also promotes understanding and appreciation of diversity, incorporating content that reflects various cultures, perspectives, and experiences.

**8. Promoting Collaboration between Schools, Families, and Communities**

• Objective: To build strong partnerships between schools, families, and the wider community to support the educational and emotional needs of students.

• Explanation: Inclusive education recognizes that education is a collaborative effort. This objective emphasizes the importance of involving families in the learning process, as well as building connections with community resources and services that can support students' holistic development. Schools are encouraged to work closely with parents, special educators, and health professionals to ensure that students receive comprehensive support.

**9. Preparing Students for Life Beyond School**

• Objective: To equip students with the academic, social, and life skills they need to succeed in further education, employment, and independent living.

• Explanation: Inclusive education aims to prepare all students for success beyond the classroom, ensuring they have the skills necessary for higher education, the workplace, and daily life. This objective focuses on helping students develop self-advocacy, critical thinking, and problem-solving skills, as well as fostering independence and resilience.

**10. Promoting Inclusive Policies and Practices**

• Objective: To encourage schools and governments to adopt policies and practices that support inclusive education at all levels.

• Explanation: Inclusive education requires systemic change, including policies that ensure all students have access to education and resources. This objective calls for the development of policies that promote inclusive practices, provide adequate funding for inclusive programs, and ensure that schools are equipped with the necessary infrastructure and resources to support diverse learners.

The objectives of inclusive education revolve around creating equitable, supportive, and adaptive learning environments where every student, regardless of their background or abilities, can thrive. By ensuring equal access, promoting collaboration, and fostering a sense of belonging, inclusive education aims to build schools and communities that celebrate diversity, enrich learning for all, and prepare students for meaningful participation in society.

### 8.1.2 Principles Of Inclusive Education

Inclusive education is built on key principles that promote equal access, participation, and learning opportunities for all students, regardless of their abilities or backgrounds. These principles serve as the foundation for designing an educational system that fosters diversity, equity, and the full development of every learner. Below is a detailed explanation of the core principles of inclusive education:

### 1. Principle of Equality and Non-Discrimination

All students, regardless of their individual characteristics, have the right to receive a quality education in an environment that is free from discrimination. Inclusive education rejects any form of exclusion based on disabilities, race, gender, socio-economic status, or other personal characteristics. This principle emphasizes that every student has an equal right to learn, and it is the responsibility of the educational system to ensure that no barriers prevent students from accessing education. Schools must provide the necessary accommodations, resources, and support to guarantee that all students can participate meaningfully in the learning process.

### 2. Principle of Diversity as a Strength

Diversity among learners is a valuable asset to the educational community, and all students should be encouraged to contribute to and benefit from this diversity. Inclusive education embraces the idea that differences in learning styles, abilities, cultural backgrounds, and experiences enrich the classroom environment. Rather than seeing diversity as a challenge, this principle highlights its role in fostering a more dynamic and engaging learning experience for all students. Teachers are encouraged to create lessons that reflect and accommodate various learning needs, and students are taught to appreciate and respect their peers' differences.

### 3. Principle of Participation and Social Inclusion

All students should be fully included in the school community and have the opportunity to participate in both academic and non-academic activities. This principle promotes the active involvement of all students in every aspect of school life, including classroom learning, extracurricular activities, sports, and social events. Inclusion is not limited to academic instruction but extends to fostering friendships and social relationships. Students with special needs or disabilities should not be isolated from their peers but rather integrated into the regular learning environment with appropriate supports.

### 4. Principle of Individualized Support and Flexibility

Educational systems must provide tailored support and use flexible teaching methods to meet the diverse needs of every student. Recognizing that students learn in different ways and at different paces, inclusive education emphasizes the need for personalized approaches. Teachers should use differentiated instruction, modify curricula when necessary, and employ various teaching strategies to accommodate diverse learners. Individualized education plans (IEPs) are often used to set specific goals and ensure that each student receives the support they need to succeed, whether through additional resources, modified assessments, or assistive technology.

### 5. Principle of Collaborative Approach

The success of inclusive education depends on the collaboration between all stakeholders, including teachers, parents, students, specialists, and the wider community. This principle highlights the importance of cooperation among educators, families, and communities to support the learning and development of all students. Teachers should work closely with special education professionals, counselors, and parents to create effective learning plans that address individual needs. Involving families in the educational process is particularly important, as it fosters stronger support systems at home and ensures that learning is continuous and holistic.

### 6. Principle of High Expectations for All

All students, regardless of their abilities or disabilities, should be held to high academic and personal development expectations. One of the cornerstones of inclusive education is the belief that all students can achieve meaningful learning outcomes when provided with the right support. Teachers must maintain high expectations for every learner, encouraging them to reach their full potential. This principle challenges the assumption that students with disabilities or learning difficulties are incapable of achieving at the same level as their peers. Instead, it emphasizes the role of educators in fostering a growth mindset and creating opportunities for success.

### 7. Principle of Respect for Human Rights

Inclusive education is grounded in the principles of human rights, particularly the right to education, participation, and equality. This principle aligns with international human rights frameworks, such as the United Nations Convention on the Rights of Persons with Disabilities (CRPD) and the Universal Declaration of Human Rights. Inclusive education recognizes that access to education is a fundamental right that cannot be denied to anyone based on their abilities. It promotes dignity, respect, and the recognition that every student has a voice in their educational journey.

## 8. Principle of Positive Attitudes and School Culture

Schools should cultivate a positive, inclusive culture where diversity is celebrated, and all students feel valued and supported. A welcoming and supportive school culture is essential for the success of inclusive education. This principle emphasizes the need for schools to actively promote inclusion by fostering positive attitudes among staff, students, and the broader school community. Training teachers and staff to understand and appreciate diversity is crucial, as well as encouraging students to develop empathy, tolerance, and mutual respect. Inclusive schools should also adopt policies and practices that reflect their commitment to diversity and equal opportunity.

## 9. Principle of Accountability and Continuous Improvement

Schools and educational systems must be held accountable for the success of inclusive education and must continuously seek ways to improve their practices. This principle emphasizes the need for schools to regularly assess their inclusive practices and ensure that they are meeting the needs of all students. Monitoring student progress, evaluating the effectiveness of support systems, and soliciting feedback from teachers, parents, and students are all crucial for ensuring that inclusive education is successful. Accountability also involves ensuring that policies and funding are in place to support inclusive initiatives and that schools are committed to making continuous improvements in their approaches to inclusion.

## 10. Principle of Universal Design for Learning (UDL)

Teaching and learning should be designed in a way that accommodates the needs of all learners from the outset, rather than adapting existing practices to meet individual needs later. Universal Design for Learning (UDL) is an educational framework that aims to make learning accessible to all students by designing lessons that are flexible and adaptable from the start. This principle encourages the use of varied teaching methods, multiple means of engagement, and flexible assessment strategies to ensure that all learners can access and succeed in the curriculum. UDL recognizes that there is no "one-size-fits-all" approach to education and promotes the idea that learning environments should be proactively inclusive of diverse needs.

The principles of inclusive education are designed to create an educational environment that is equitable, diverse, and supportive of all learners. By emphasizing equality, collaboration, respect for diversity, individualized support, and high expectations, inclusive education seeks to ensure that every student has the opportunity to succeed. These principles guide the development of teaching practices, school policies, and educational frameworks that foster an inclusive, welcoming, and productive learning environment for all students.

### 8.1.3 Importance of Inclusive Education

Inclusive education is of immense importance in today's educational landscape, as it seeks to provide equitable learning opportunities for all students, regardless of their abilities, backgrounds, or socio-economic status.

### 1. Promotes Equality and Equity

One of the fundamental goals of inclusive education is to ensure that all students have access to the same quality of education, regardless of their differences. It promotes equity by recognizing and addressing the diverse needs of students, ensuring that everyone has an equal opportunity to succeed. By eliminating discrimination based on disability, gender, race, or social background, inclusive education creates a more just and fair educational environment. This contributes to reducing societal inequalities, as education is often the most significant tool for upward mobility. When all students receive the support they need, they are better equipped to overcome social or economic barriers later in life.

### 2. Encourages Social Integration

Inclusive education brings together students from diverse backgrounds and with different abilities in the same learning environment, promoting social cohesion. It allows students to interact, cooperate, and learn from one another, fostering mutual understanding and respect. By growing up in an inclusive environment, students are more likely to become empathetic and open-minded adults who value diversity and inclusivity in broader society. This interaction helps in breaking down stereotypes and misconceptions about individuals with disabilities or from marginalized communities. It builds a foundation for a more inclusive society where differences are embraced rather than stigmatized.

### 3. Improves Academic and Social Outcomes

Inclusive education benefits both students with and without disabilities. Research has shown that when students with special needs are educated alongside their peers in a well-supported inclusive environment, they experience higher academic outcomes. This is because they have access to the general curriculum, higher expectations, and a stimulating peer environment. For students without disabilities, inclusive education fosters a richer learning environment. Exposure to diversity enhances their social skills, such as empathy, problem-solving, and collaboration, which are critical in both personal and professional life.

### 4. Fosters Personal Growth and Development

Inclusive education supports the holistic development of all students. It ensures that learning is not only about academic achievement but also about personal growth, emotional development, and social skills. Students in inclusive environments learn to respect individual differences, work collaboratively, and build meaningful relationships with peers of different abilities and backgrounds. This experience contributes to the development of well-rounded individuals who are more adaptive, resilient, and prepared for real-world challenges. It helps in fostering independence, self-esteem, and a sense of belonging among all students.

### 5. Reduces Segregation and Stigmatization

In traditional education systems, students with disabilities or learning difficulties are often placed in separate classrooms or schools, leading to isolation and stigma. Inclusive education challenges this by integrating students of all abilities into mainstream classrooms, with appropriate support and accommodations. This reduces the psychological impact of being "different" and promotes a sense of community and inclusion for all students. It normalizes the presence of diverse abilities within the classroom and helps prevent the negative effects of labeling and segregation.

### 6. Builds a Culture of Collaboration

Inclusive education requires collaboration between educators, specialists, parents, and the community. Teachers work with support staff, such as special education professionals and counselors, to meet the needs of all students. This collaborative approach strengthens the entire educational system by fostering a team-based mentality and shared responsibility for student success. This collaboration promotes innovation in teaching practices and creates a more dynamic and supportive learning environment. Teachers learn to adapt their methods to accommodate a wide range of learning styles, making education more flexible and responsive to student needs.

### 7. Prepares Students for Life Beyond School

Inclusive education equips students with the skills they need to succeed in a diverse and interconnected world. By learning alongside peers of different abilities and backgrounds, students develop critical life skills, such as empathy, cooperation, adaptability, and problem-solving. These skills are essential in higher education, the workplace, and society. Inclusive education prepares students to thrive in diverse environments, helping them become responsible, respectful, and inclusive citizens.

## 8. Complies with International Human Rights and Legal Obligations

Inclusive education aligns with global human rights standards, such as the United Nations Convention on the Rights of Persons with Disabilities (CRPD) and the Universal Declaration of Human Rights, which affirm that every individual has the right to an education without discrimination. By implementing inclusive education policies, countries fulfill their legal and moral obligations to provide equal access to education. This contributes to global efforts to create a more inclusive, equitable, and rights-based society.

## 9. Promotes Lifelong Learning and Inclusivity in Society

By fostering an inclusive mindset from an early age, schools can instill values that promote lifelong learning, inclusivity, and respect for diversity. Students who grow up in inclusive educational settings are more likely to carry these values into their adult lives, influencing how they engage in their communities, workplaces, and relationships. Inclusive education plants the seeds for a more inclusive and equitable society. Students who experience inclusion firsthand are more likely to advocate for the rights of others and to contribute to building communities that embrace diversity and provide equal opportunities for all.

## 10. Enhances Teacher Development and Skills

Inclusive education requires educators to develop a broader set of skills, including differentiated instruction, classroom management, and the ability to accommodate diverse learning needs. This leads to improved teaching practices that benefit all students, not just those with special needs. Teachers become more effective and adaptable, and schools become more flexible in responding to individual student needs. This leads to better educational outcomes overall, as teachers are equipped to engage all students in meaningful learning experiences.

The importance of inclusive education lies in its ability to create equitable and supportive learning environments that cater to the needs of every student. By promoting equality, fostering social integration, improving academic outcomes, and building a more inclusive society, inclusive education ensures that all students can thrive, both academically and personally. It prepares individuals for life beyond school, helping them develop the skills, values, and mindsets necessary to navigate a diverse and complex world. Moreover, inclusive education helps fulfill international human rights obligations, contributing to a more just and equal global society.

## 8.2 Socially Disadvantaged Children

**Meaning and Concept of Socially Disadvantaged Children**

Socially disadvantaged children are those who face significant barriers to their education, well-being, and development due to socio-economic, cultural, or environmental factors. These children often grow up in conditions that limit their access to essential resources such as quality education, healthcare, housing, and emotional support. The disadvantages they experience may stem from poverty, discrimination, disabilities, or unstable family environments, among other factors.

The concept of being *"socially disadvantaged"* refers to the structural inequalities that prevent these children from having the same opportunities as their more advantaged peers. Social disadvantage is not solely about economic poverty but includes factors such as social exclusion, marginalization, and systemic barriers that restrict children's ability to achieve their full potential.

**Definitions of Socially Disadvantaged Children**

**1. UNESCO:** Socially disadvantaged children are defined as those who are "deprived of adequate educational opportunities due to factors such as poverty, disabilities, gender discrimination, geographic isolation, and other socio-cultural factors, making it difficult for them to participate fully in society."

**2. World Bank:** The World Bank defines socially disadvantaged children as "those who face significant challenges in achieving educational outcomes due to economic hardship, marginalization, or living in underserved areas, resulting in limited access to quality schooling and developmental support."

**3. National Association of Social Workers (NASW):** "Socially disadvantaged children are individuals who, due to socioeconomic factors, experience barriers to their emotional, educational, and social development, often resulting in lower academic performance and reduced life opportunities."

**4.** In the Words of **Dr. James Heckman, Nobel Laureate in Economics:** "Children from socially disadvantaged backgrounds face hurdles that limit their ability to develop the essential cognitive and social skills needed for success in life. Early intervention and access to quality education can mitigate these challenges."

## Importance of Recognizing Social Disadvantage

Recognizing social disadvantage is crucial for building an equitable society where all individuals, regardless of their backgrounds, have the opportunity to thrive. Social disadvantage refers to the structural barriers and inequalities that prevent individuals, particularly children, from accessing resources and opportunities necessary for their development and success. Understanding and acknowledging these disadvantages is the first step in addressing them effectively. Below is explained why recognizing social disadvantage is important:

### 1. Promotes Equality and Fairness

Recognizing social disadvantage helps to ensure that everyone has an equal opportunity to succeed. Children from disadvantaged backgrounds often start life at a significant disadvantage compared to their peers. Without recognition of these challenges, policies and interventions may inadvertently perpetuate inequality.

• Impact: Once identified, schools, governments, and organizations can implement targeted interventions to support those who need it most. This levels the playing field, allowing disadvantaged children to have the same opportunities as others.

### 2. Improves Educational Outcomes

Children facing social disadvantages, such as poverty, discrimination, or family instability, often struggle in school due to a lack of resources and support. Recognizing these challenges allows educators to provide tailored support, such as access to free meals, counseling, tutoring, or inclusive education programs.

• Impact: When social disadvantage is addressed, children are more likely to stay in school, perform better academically, and develop the skills needed for future success. This leads to better life outcomes and higher social mobility.

### 3. Reduces Poverty and Social Exclusion

Social disadvantage is often a key factor in the perpetuation of poverty and social exclusion. Children born into disadvantaged families are more likely to remain disadvantaged throughout their lives. Recognizing these patterns helps policymakers design interventions that break the cycle of poverty, such as improving access to education, healthcare, and housing.

• Impact: By addressing the root causes of social disadvantage, societies can reduce poverty levels and create more inclusive communities where everyone has a chance to contribute and succeed.

### 4. Fosters Social Cohesion

When the needs of socially disadvantaged children are recognized and addressed, it fosters a sense of belonging and inclusion. Ignoring social disadvantage often leads to marginalization, which can result in social tensions, crime, and political instability. Recognizing the issue allows for the creation of more cohesive societies that value and support all members, regardless of their backgrounds.

• Impact: Social cohesion leads to more peaceful, stable communities where individuals feel valued and connected. This benefits everyone by creating stronger social bonds and reducing the likelihood of social unrest.

### 5. Supports Holistic Child Development

Socially disadvantaged children often face multiple challenges, including poor health, inadequate nutrition, emotional stress, and lack of educational resources. Recognizing these disadvantages allows for a holistic approach to child development, where physical, emotional, and cognitive needs are met through targeted support programs.

• Impact: Children who receive comprehensive support are more likely to develop into healthy, well-rounded adults. This reduces the likelihood of long-term negative outcomes, such as unemployment, mental health issues, or criminal behavior.

### 6. Informs Better Policy Making

Policies that do not take social disadvantage into account are unlikely to be effective in addressing the needs of the most vulnerable. Recognizing social disadvantage ensures that policies are evidence-based and targeted toward those who need the most support.

• Impact: Policies informed by an understanding of social disadvantage lead to more efficient allocation of resources and more effective solutions. For example, targeted educational programs, social welfare systems, and healthcare initiatives can improve outcomes for disadvantaged groups, ultimately benefiting society as a whole.

### 7. Enhances Teacher and Educator Awareness

Teachers and educators play a vital role in the lives of socially disadvantaged children. By recognizing the specific challenges these children face, educators can adapt their teaching methods and provide the necessary support to ensure these students succeed.

• Impact: When educators are aware of social disadvantage, they can create more inclusive, supportive classroom environments. This leads to better engagement, higher academic achievement, and improved social-emotional development for disadvantaged students.

Recognizing social disadvantage is essential for creating an inclusive, equitable society where every child has the opportunity to succeed. By identifying and addressing the barriers that socially disadvantaged children face, we can promote equality, improve educational and life outcomes, reduce poverty, foster social cohesion, and break the cycle of disadvantage. Ultimately, addressing social disadvantage benefits both individuals and society as a whole, leading to stronger, more just communities.

### 8.2.1 Characteristics of Socially Disadvantaged

Socially disadvantaged children face various challenges that stem from their environment, socio-economic conditions, and systemic inequalities. These challenges manifest in different aspects of their lives, affecting their education, social development, and overall well-being. The key characteristics of socially disadvantaged children:

**1. Limited Access to Resources**

Socially disadvantaged children often come from low-income families, which limits their access to basic needs like nutritious food, quality education, healthcare, and even safe housing. This lack of resources affects their physical, emotional, and cognitive development, leading to issues such as malnutrition, poor health, and lower academic performance.

**2. Educational Challenges**

These children often attend under-resourced schools or live in areas where quality education is not readily available. They may also have fewer educational materials at home and limited parental support for academic activities. As a result, they are more likely to experience academic difficulties, struggle with learning, and have higher dropout rates compared to their peers.

**3. Social Exclusion and Marginalization**

Children from marginalized communities, such as ethnic or racial minorities, children with disabilities, or those from migrant families, often face discrimination, bullying, or social exclusion in school and society. This can lead to feelings of isolation, low self-esteem, and a lack of belonging, further hindering their social and emotional development.

**4. Unstable Family Background**

Socially disadvantaged children are more likely to come from unstable family situations, such as single-parent households, families dealing with unemployment, domestic violence, or substance abuse.These unstable environments create emotional and psychological stress, affecting the child's ability to focus on school, form healthy relationships, and engage positively with their surroundings.

### 5. Lower Aspirations and Motivation

Due to constant exposure to poverty and social limitations, many socially disadvantaged children develop lower aspirations for the future. They may feel discouraged or believe they are less likely to succeed academically or professionally. This mindset can negatively influence their motivation to pursue education or other opportunities for personal growth, perpetuating the cycle of disadvantage.

### 6. Health and Well-being Issues

Socially disadvantaged children often face health problems due to inadequate healthcare, poor nutrition, and exposure to unsafe living conditions. They are also more vulnerable to mental health issues such as anxiety and depression. Poor health negatively affects their concentration, learning, and participation in school activities, making it harder for them to achieve academic success.

### 7. Increased Exposure to Violence and Crime

Many disadvantaged children live in neighborhoods with higher rates of crime and violence. They may witness or experience domestic violence, gang activity, or unsafe community environments. Exposure to violence can lead to trauma, behavioral issues, and a heightened risk of engaging in delinquent behaviors themselves, which further isolates them from mainstream society.

### 8. Language and Cultural Barriers

For children from immigrant or minority communities, language barriers and cultural differences can make it difficult to fully integrate into school systems. They may struggle to understand lessons or face prejudice due to their cultural background.These barriers can hinder academic progress, make it difficult to form friendships, and increase feelings of alienation.

### 9. Reduced Access to Extracurricular Activities

Due to financial constraints, socially disadvantaged children often lack opportunities to participate in extracurricular activities such as sports, arts, or after-school programs that promote personal development and social skills.The absence of such activities limits their exposure to positive social networks, skill-building opportunities, and personal interests that could enhance their confidence and future prospects.

### 10. Frequent Relocation and School Changes

Families facing financial instability or homelessness may frequently move, leading to school changes and disruptions in the child's education. Frequent relocation makes it harder for children to build stable relationships with teachers and peers, maintain academic consistency, and feel a sense of stability.

### 11. Emotional and Behavioral Issues

Socially disadvantaged children often struggle with emotional regulation due to stress, trauma, or neglect in their personal lives. This may manifest as anxiety, anger, or withdrawal in school settings. Emotional and behavioral issues can disrupt learning, lead to disciplinary problems, and further isolate the child from their peers and academic success.

### 12. Limited Parental Involvement

Parents of socially disadvantaged children are often less involved in their children's education due to long working hours, lack of education, or stressful life circumstances. This lack of involvement can reduce the child's support system, making it harder for them to stay engaged with schoolwork and leading to lower academic achievement.

Socially disadvantaged children face a range of challenges that affect their academic, social, and emotional development. These children often deal with limited access to resources, educational challenges, social exclusion, and unstable family environments, which can significantly hinder their progress. Recognizing these characteristics is essential for providing targeted interventions and support systems that can help break the cycle of disadvantage and give these children the opportunity to succeed.

### 8.3 Learning Disability

*Learning disabilities* are neurological disorders that affect the brain's ability to process, store, retrieve, and respond to information. These disabilities make it difficult for individuals to learn in traditional ways, despite having average or above-average intelligence. Learning disabilities can affect various areas of learning, including reading, writing, math, reasoning, and social skills. Unlike intellectual disabilities, learning disabilities do not stem from a lack of effort, motivation, or environmental factors, but rather from how the brain processes information.

Understanding learning disabilities is crucial because it allows educators, parents, and policymakers to provide appropriate interventions and accommodations that help children and adults with learning disabilities succeed in academic, professional, and personal contexts. By addressing the unique needs of those with learning disabilities, we can create inclusive learning environments that foster the strengths and talents of every individual.

**Impact of Learning Disabilities**

*1. Academic Performance:* Children with learning disabilities often struggle with basic academic skills, such as reading, writing, and math. This can lead to frustration, poor self-esteem, and disengagement from school if not addressed early.

*2. Social and Emotional Development:* Many children with learning disabilities face difficulties in social settings, including understanding social cues, making friends, or managing emotions. These challenges can lead to feelings of isolation or depression.

*3. Long-Term Consequences:* Without the right support, individuals with learning disabilities may have trouble finding and keeping jobs, managing daily life tasks, or maintaining relationships. However, with proper intervention and support, many can lead successful, fulfilling lives.

*4. Intervention and Support:* Early diagnosis and intervention are key to managing learning disabilities. Special education services, individualized education plans (IEPs), and classroom accommodations, such as extra time for tests or alternative teaching methods, can help children overcome barriers to learning.

*5. Inclusive Education:* Schools play a vital role in creating inclusive environments where students with learning disabilities can thrive alongside their peers. Tailoring education to meet their needs not only improves academic outcomes but also builds their confidence and social skills.

**Meaning and Concept of Learning Disability**

A learning disability is a neurological disorder that affects the way an individual's brain processes information. It can hinder the ability to understand or use spoken or written language, perform mathematical calculations, coordinate movements, or direct attention. Importantly, a learning disability is not linked to intelligence; individuals with learning disabilities typically have average or above-average intelligence but struggle with specific types of learning.

Learning disabilities are not a singular, defined condition; instead, they encompass a broad spectrum of difficulties that interfere with specific academic and developmental skills. These disabilities are intrinsic to the individual, meaning they are due to differences in brain function. Learning disabilities are lifelong conditions, but their impact can be mitigated with appropriate support and teaching strategies.

**Definitions of Learning Disability**

1. National Center for Learning Disabilities (NCLD): *"Learning disabilities are neurological disorders that can make it difficult to acquire certain academic and social skills. They affect the brain's ability to process, store, and respond to information."*

2. The Individuals with Disabilities Education Act (IDEA), U.S.: *"A learning disability is a disorder in one or more of the basic psychological processes involved in understanding or in using language, spoken or written, which may manifest itself in an imperfect ability to listen, think, speak, read, write, spell, or do mathematical calculations."*

3. British Dyslexia Association: *"A specific learning difficulty, such as dyslexia, is a condition that affects the way information is learned and processed. It can result in problems with learning and skills development, particularly in reading, writing, and spelling."*

4. World Health Organization (WHO): *"Learning disabilities are disorders that affect the ability to learn in a typical manner, despite normal intelligence and conventional instruction. These disabilities can affect the acquisition and use of listening, speaking, reading, writing, reasoning, or mathematical abilities."*

Learning disabilities are lifelong challenges that require understanding, proper intervention, and support from educators, families, and society. By recognizing that learning disabilities are rooted in how the brain processes information, we can move away from stigmatizing individuals who struggle academically and instead focus on providing them with the necessary tools and accommodations to succeed. Early diagnosis and individualized strategies can significantly improve outcomes for those with learning disabilities, helping them to unlock their potential and lead productive, fulfilling lives.

### 8.3.1 Classification Of Learning Disabilities Along Characteristics

Learning disabilities are generally classified based on the specific areas of learning that are affected. These classifications help educators and professionals design targeted interventions to address the unique challenges faced by individuals with these disabilities.

Broadly, learning disabilities can be grouped into three main categories: *dyslexia* (related to reading and language processing), *dysgraphia* (related to writing), and *dyscalculia* (related to math). Additionally, learning disabilities also include challenges related to auditory and visual processing.

A Comprehensive classification of learning disabilities are as under:

### 1. Dyslexia (Reading Disabilities)

Dyslexia is a learning disability that primarily affects reading and language-based processing skills. It impacts the ability to decode words, read fluently, and comprehend written text.

• *Characteristics:*

• Difficulty with phonological processing (understanding the relationship between letters and sounds). • Trouble decoding words and recognizing sight words.

• Slow reading speed and poor reading comprehension.

• Difficulty with spelling and written expression.

• Examples: Misreading words, reversing letters (such as 'b' and 'd'), skipping words while reading, or reading below expected grade level.

### 2. Dysgraphia (Writing Disabilities)

Dysgraphia affects the ability to write coherently. Individuals with this disability may struggle with handwriting, spelling, organizing their thoughts, and constructing meaningful sentences.

• *Characteristics:*

• Illegible handwriting with inconsistent letter size and spacing.

• Poor spelling and grammar. • Difficulty organizing written thoughts coherently.

• Challenges with fine motor skills, making it hard to hold a pencil or form letters.

• Examples: Difficulty writing neatly, inability to follow the structure of an essay, poor spelling, and problems copying text from the board.

### 3. Dyscalculia (Math Disabilities)

Dyscalculia is a learning disability that impacts the ability to understand numbers and mathematical concepts. Individuals with dyscalculia may struggle with basic arithmetic, problem solving, and understanding number relationships.

• *Characteristics:*

• Difficulty understanding numerical concepts, such as quantities and the relationship between numbers.

• Challenges with basic arithmetic operations (addition, subtraction, multiplication, division). • Problems understanding time, patterns, or sequences.

• Trouble with abstract mathematical concepts such as algebra or geometry.

• Examples: Inability to remember math facts, difficulty with counting, or struggling with time management (e.g., reading clocks or calendars).

**4. Auditory Processing Disorder (APD)**

APD affects how the brain processes auditory information. Individuals with this disorder have difficulty interpreting and processing sounds, even though their hearing ability is normal.

• *Characteristics:*

• Difficulty distinguishing between similar sounds (e.g., 'b' and 'p' sounds).

• Trouble following spoken instructions, especially in noisy environments.

• Difficulty understanding rapid speech or multi-step instructions. • Frequently asking for repetition or clarification.

• Examples: Struggling to follow conversations in noisy places or misinterpreting spoken words, which can affect learning, particularly in language-based subjects.

**5. Visual Processing Disorder (VPD)**

Visual processing disorder affects how the brain interprets visual information. This can impact reading, writing, and the ability to understand visual patterns or spatial relationships.

• *Characteristics:*

• Difficulty distinguishing between different shapes, letters, or symbols.

• Trouble with visual-spatial tasks, such as understanding maps or graphs.

• Problems tracking text while reading, leading to skipping words or lines.

• Inability to process non-verbal information, such as body language or facial expressions.

• Examples: Confusing similar-looking letters (e.g., 'p' and 'q'), difficulty copying shapes or graphs, or trouble reading charts and diagrams.

**6. Non-Verbal Learning Disability (NVLD)**

NVLD is a learning disability that primarily affects non-verbal reasoning, social skills, and spatial awareness. Individuals with NVLD may excel in verbal tasks but struggle with social cues, physical coordination, and visual-spatial tasks.

• *Characteristics:*

• Strong verbal skills but difficulty understanding non-verbal communication (e.g., body language, facial expressions).

• Poor hand-eye coordination, difficulty with puzzles, or problems with fine motor skills.

• Trouble interpreting abstract concepts and visual-spatial relationships (e.g., maps or graphs).

• Social challenges, such as misreading social cues or difficulty making friends.

• Examples: Struggling to read body language during conversations, difficulty with sports or other physical activities, or challenges with visual memory.

## 7. Language Processing Disorder (LPD)

LPD affects the ability to understand or produce spoken language. It impacts both receptive (understanding language) and expressive (speaking) skills.

• *Characteristics:*

• Difficulty following spoken instructions or comprehending complex language structures.

• Problems organizing thoughts when speaking or expressing ideas clearly.

• Challenges with vocabulary, sentence structure, and grammar.

• May struggle with learning new words or following multi-step directions.

• Examples: Inability to follow verbal explanations, struggling to express ideas coherently, or confusion with understanding words in context.

## 8. Attention Deficit Hyperactivity Disorder (ADHD)

While not classified as a learning disability itself, ADHD can significantly impact learning by affecting focus, attention, and self-regulation. Many children with ADHD also have co-occurring learning disabilities.

• *Characteristics:*

• Inattention: Difficulty focusing on tasks, listening, or following instructions.

• Hyperactivity: Restlessness, fidgeting, or excessive movement.

• Impulsivity: Difficulty waiting for turns, interrupting others, or making hasty decisions.

• Examples: Struggling to complete assignments, easily distracted, or difficulty following structured lessons.

Learning disabilities can present in various forms, each affecting specific aspects of learning, such as reading, writing, math, language, or processing auditory or visual information. Understanding the different classifications of learning disabilities allows educators and parents to identify the most effective strategies and interventions to support students with these challenges. Early diagnosis and tailored support are essential for helping individuals with learning disabilities succeed academically, socially, and professionally.

## 8.4 Educational Provisions

Inclusive education focuses on ensuring that all students, regardless of their abilities or disabilities, receive a quality education within the general education system. To achieve this, various educational provisions are designed to meet the diverse needs of learners in an inclusive setting. These provisions aim to remove barriers to learning and ensure that students with disabilities or special needs can fully participate and succeed in mainstream classrooms.

Key educational provisions that support inclusive education:

### 1. Individualized Education Plans (IEPs)

An Individualized Education Plan (IEP) is a legal document created for students with disabilities that outlines specific educational goals, accommodations, and support services tailored to their unique needs.

· *Purpose:*

· To provide a customized learning experience for each student, addressing their specific strengths and challenges.

· To ensure that students receive necessary accommodations and modifications to succeed in general education classrooms.

· *Key Components:*

· Clear academic and developmental goals for the student.

· Details about the services and accommodations the student will receive (e.g., extra time for tests, modified assignments).

· Regular assessments and reviews to monitor progress.

· Example: A student with dyslexia might have an IEP that provides accommodations such as audiobooks, extra time for tests, and one-on-one reading support.

### 2. Support Services and Specialized Staff

Inclusive education requires the involvement of specialized staff, such as special education teachers, speech therapists, and occupational therapists, who provide support to students with special needs.

· *Purpose:*

· To ensure that students with disabilities receive the necessary expertise and assistance in areas where they struggle.

• To provide additional support to general education teachers to help them effectively teach students with diverse learning needs.

• *Key Components:*

• Collaboration between general education teachers and special education staff to develop and implement individualized learning strategies.

• Regular therapy sessions for students who require speech, physical, or occupational support.

• In-class support from teacher aides or paraprofessionals who assist students with disabilities in staying engaged with the lesson.

• Example: A student with motor difficulties might receive assistance from an occupational therapist who helps them with handwriting and fine motor skills.

### 3. Classroom Accommodations

Classroom accommodations refer to modifications or supports provided to students to help them access the curriculum and demonstrate their knowledge and skills.

• *Purpose:*

• To remove barriers to learning by adapting the learning environment or instructional methods to meet students' needs.

• To ensure that students with disabilities have the same opportunity to succeed as their peers without disabilities.

• *Key Components:*

• Adjustments in teaching materials (e.g., larger print, braille, or simplified text).

• Use of assistive technology, such as speech-to-text software, hearing aids, or augmentative communication devices.

• Allowing extra time for assignments and tests or providing alternative methods for completing assessments (e.g., oral exams).

• Example: A student with a visual impairment might use large-print textbooks and text-to-speech software to access reading materials.

### 4. Curriculum Adaptation and Differentiated Instruction

Curriculum adaptation involves modifying the content, teaching strategies, and assessment methods to meet the diverse needs of all learners. Differentiated instruction refers to teaching techniques that address the varying abilities and learning styles within a classroom.

• *Purpose:*

• To make the curriculum accessible and engaging for students with different learning needs.

• To ensure that all students, regardless of their abilities, can meet the educational objectives and progress academically.

• *Key Components:*

• Modifying lessons to include multi-sensory approaches (e.g., visual aids, hands-on activities, and audio resources).

• Offering students different ways to demonstrate their understanding (e.g., written essays, presentations, or creative projects).

• Creating flexible grouping in the classroom, where students work in different groups based on their learning preferences and skill levels.

• Example: In a science class, a student with a learning disability might receive hands-on experiments and visual aids to reinforce concepts, while a student who excels may work on more complex, independent projects.

## 5. Universal Design for Learning (UDL)

Universal Design for Learning (UDL) is an educational framework that guides the development of flexible learning environments that can accommodate the needs of all learners, including those with disabilities.

• *Purpose:*

• To provide multiple means of representation, engagement, and expression to ensure that the curriculum is accessible to all students.

• To proactively remove barriers in the learning environment, making education inclusive from the start.

• *Key Components:*

• Multiple Means of Representation: Presenting information in various formats (e.g., text, audio, video) to cater to different learning styles.

• Multiple Means of Engagement: Providing students with different ways to engage with the material, such as collaborative projects, individual work, or interactive activities.

• Multiple Means of Expression: Allowing students to demonstrate what they have learned in different ways (e.g., tests, creative projects, verbal presentations).

• Example: In a history lesson, students may choose to watch a documentary, read a book, or listen to a podcast, depending on their preferred learning style, and can express their understanding through a written report, a group presentation, or an artwork.

## 6. Inclusive Assessment Practices

Inclusive assessment refers to the practice of assessing students' progress in a way that takes into account their diverse abilities and learning needs.

• *Purpose:*

• To provide fair and accurate assessments of students' knowledge and skills, without being hindered by their disabilities.

• To ensure that all students can demonstrate their learning in a way that is equitable and accessible.

• *Key Components:*

• Providing alternative forms of assessment, such as oral presentations, practical demonstrations, or digital portfolios.

• Allowing extended time, providing breaks during testing, or offering a quiet testing environment for students with attention or sensory difficulties.

• Using formative assessments (ongoing feedback) rather than solely relying on high-stakes summative assessments (final exams).

• Example: A student with a learning disability might be assessed through a portfolio of their work over time, rather than through a single standardized test.

## 7. Peer Support and Collaborative Learning

Peer support and collaborative learning involve the integration of students with and without disabilities working together in the classroom to promote inclusion and foster social skills.

• *Purpose:*

• To encourage positive peer interactions and build a sense of community and belonging among all students.

• To provide natural supports, where students with disabilities can learn from and collaborate with their peers.

• *Key Components:*

• Implementing buddy systems, where students are paired with a peer to help with academic tasks or social integration.

• Encouraging group work, where students of different abilities collaborate on projects, sharing knowledge and skills.

• Promoting peer tutoring, where students with specific strengths help their classmates in areas of difficulty.

• Example: A student with autism might be paired with a classmate to help navigate social situations during group activities, enhancing their social skills and sense of inclusion.

## 8. Parental Involvement and Advocacy

Parental involvement refers to the active participation of parents in the educational planning and decision-making processes for their children with disabilities.

· *Purpose*:

· To ensure that parents have a voice in their child's education and that their insights and concerns are incorporated into the child's learning plan.

· To promote a collaborative relationship between parents and educators in supporting the child's development.

· *Key Components*:

· Regular communication between parents and teachers regarding the child's progress and any necessary adjustments to their learning plan.

· Encouraging parents to participate in IEP meetings and advocate for accommodations and services that their child needs.

· Providing resources and support to help parents assist their child's learning at home.

· Example: A parent might work with teachers to ensure that a student with ADHD receives appropriate classroom accommodations, such as a quiet work environment or extra time for tests.

Inclusive education requires a multi-faceted approach to ensure that all students, regardless of their abilities or disabilities, have equal opportunities to succeed. Through individualized education plans, classroom accommodations, curriculum adaptations, and support from specialized staff, schools can create environments where every student feels valued and included. These educational provisions are essential for fostering academic achievement, social development, and personal growth in students with diverse needs, ultimately leading to more equitable and inclusive educational systems.

### 8.4.1 Role of Teacher

The role of the teacher in inclusive education is crucial to creating a learning environment where all students, regardless of their abilities or backgrounds, can thrive. Teachers are not just responsible for delivering subject content; they play a pivotal role in fostering an inclusive, supportive, and equitable classroom that accommodates diverse learners. Below is an elaboration on the different roles and responsibilities teachers have in the context of inclusive education:

### 1. Facilitator of Learning

In an inclusive classroom, the teacher acts as a facilitator who guides and supports all students in their learning processes. Rather than being a one-size-fits-all instructor, the teacher adapts lessons to meet the diverse needs of students, ensuring that each one has access to the curriculum.

• Designing and delivering lessons that are accessible to students with a range of abilities.

• Using differentiated instruction techniques, such as adjusting the level of difficulty or providing multiple ways for students to engage with the material.

• Encouraging active participation from all students, ensuring that no one feels left out or marginalized.

• Example: A teacher might incorporate visual aids, hands-on activities, and technology to ensure that students with varying learning styles can all engage with the material in ways that suit their strengths.

## 2. Adapting and Modifying Curriculum

Teachers in an inclusive setting must tailor the curriculum to meet the individual needs of their students. This requires flexibility and creativity to ensure that students with disabilities or other learning challenges can still achieve the educational goals set for them.

• Modifying lesson plans, assignments, and assessments to suit students' abilities without compromising the integrity of the curriculum.

• Incorporating assistive technology and alternative learning materials (e.g., audiobooks, digital content) to support students with disabilities.

• Collaborating with special education teachers to develop Individualized Education Plans (IEPs) and ensure their implementation in the classroom.

• Example: A teacher might modify a written assignment into a verbal presentation for a student with dysgraphia, allowing them to demonstrate their understanding without being hindered by their writing difficulty.

## 3. Creating an Inclusive Classroom Environment

The teacher is responsible for fostering an inclusive classroom environment that promotes respect, empathy, and collaboration among all students. A positive and supportive atmosphere helps students with disabilities or social disadvantages feel accepted and valued.

• Promoting social inclusion by encouraging group work and peer support, where students of different abilities collaborate and learn from one another.

• Setting clear expectations for respect and empathy, and actively addressing any form of bullying or exclusion.

• Celebrating diversity by incorporating diverse cultural, linguistic, and ability perspectives into the classroom.

• Example: A teacher might pair students with and without disabilities to work on a group project, encouraging peer support and fostering a sense of community within the classroom.

## 4. Supporter of Social and Emotional Development

Teachers play a key role in supporting the social and emotional well-being of students, particularly those who may struggle with disabilities, learning difficulties, or social disadvantages. Building a student's self-esteem and emotional resilience is an essential part of inclusive education.

• Providing emotional support and encouragement to students who may feel frustrated or overwhelmed by academic challenges.

• Teaching and modeling social skills, conflict resolution, and emotional regulation to help students navigate the social aspects of school life.

• Encouraging students to take pride in their unique strengths and abilities, and to see their challenges as opportunities for growth.

• Example: A teacher might hold regular classroom meetings where students discuss their feelings and work through conflicts, helping build emotional intelligence and a strong classroom community.

## 5. Collaborator with Special Education Staff and Parents

Collaboration is key in inclusive education, and teachers must work closely with special education staff, paraprofessionals, and parents to ensure that students receive the support they need.

• Working with special education professionals to develop and implement Individualized Education Plans (IEPs) and provide tailored interventions.

• Communicating regularly with parents about their child's progress, challenges, and strategies for supporting learning at home.

• Engaging in team meetings to discuss the progress of students with disabilities, adjust strategies as needed, and ensure that the student is receiving the right support.

• Example: A teacher might collaborate with a speech therapist to incorporate speech and language goals into classroom activities for a student with communication difficulties.

## 6. Advocate for Inclusion

Teachers are not only responsible for implementing inclusive practices within their own classrooms, but they also act as advocates for inclusive education at the school and community levels.

• Advocating for the needs of students with disabilities or learning challenges in school policy discussions.

• Promoting professional development for themselves and their colleagues to stay informed about best practices in inclusive education.

• Educating other students, parents, and staff about the importance of inclusion and creating a supportive environment for all learners.

• Example: A teacher might push for school-wide training on Universal Design for Learning (UDL) principles, ensuring that all staff are equipped to create accessible learning experiences for diverse students.

## 7. Continual Professional Development

Inclusive education requires teachers to continuously develop their skills and knowledge about how to best support students with diverse needs. Teachers must stay informed about new strategies, tools, and resources that can help them create more inclusive classrooms.

• Participating in ongoing professional development courses, workshops, and seminars on special education, inclusive teaching strategies, and the latest research.

• Staying updated on legal requirements and rights of students with disabilities to ensure compliance with educational policies and laws.

• Reflecting on their own teaching practices, seeking feedback, and making adjustments to better serve all students.

• Example: A teacher might attend a workshop on differentiated instruction to learn new ways of engaging students with a range of abilities and learning styles.

## 8. Promoter of Equal Opportunities

In an inclusive classroom, the teacher ensures that all students have equal access to learning opportunities. This means that students with disabilities or learning difficulties should not be excluded from any activities, and should have access to the same learning experiences as their peers.

• Providing necessary accommodations or modifications so that all students can participate in classroom activities, assessments, and extracurriculars.

• Ensuring that learning materials and resources are accessible to all students, regardless of their abilities.

• Promoting high expectations for all students, recognizing that every student has the potential to succeed with the right support.

• Example: A teacher might ensure that students with physical disabilities have access to adaptive sports equipment so that they can participate in physical education classes alongside their peers.

The role of a teacher in inclusive education is multifaceted, requiring flexibility, creativity, and empathy. Teachers must be prepared to adapt their teaching methods, collaborate with support staff and parents, advocate for the needs of students with disabilities, and create a welcoming environment where all students feel valued and capable of success. By fostering a culture of inclusion, teachers help build a classroom where every student has the opportunity to learn, grow, and thrive academically, socially, and emotionally.

# Key Terms

**Key terms commonly used in Peace education:**

- **Conflict resolution:** *The process of addressing and resolving conflicts in nonviolent and constructive ways, often through negotiation, mediation, or dialogue.*
- **Nonviolence:** *The principle and practice of using peaceful means to resolve conflicts, reject violence, and promote social justice and human rights.*
- **Intercultural understanding:** *The ability to appreciate and respect diverse cultures, beliefs, and perspectives, fostering empathy, tolerance, and dialogue among different groups.*
- **Human rights:** *The fundamental rights and freedoms that all individuals are entitled to, such as the right to life, liberty, equality, and dignity. Peace education emphasizes the promotion and protection of human rights.*
- **Global citizenship:** *The recognition of interconnectedness and shared responsibility among individuals, communities, and nations in addressing global challenges and promoting peace, justice, and sustainability.*
- **Social justice:** *The pursuit of fair and equitable treatment of all individuals and groups, challenging systems of discrimination, oppression, and inequality.*
- **Gender equality:** *The principle of equal rights, opportunities, and treatment for individuals of all genders, addressing gender-based discrimination, stereotypes, and violence.*
- **Active listening:** *A communication skill that involves fully focusing on and understanding the speaker's perspective, promoting empathy, dialogue, and mutual understanding.*
- **Empathy:** *The ability to understand and share the feelings, experiences, and perspectives of others, promoting compassion, care, and connection.*
- **Mediation:** *A process of facilitating dialogue and negotiation between conflicting parties by a neutral third party, aiming to find mutually acceptable solutions and restore relationships.*
- **Peacebuilding:** *The active and long-term process of preventing conflicts, addressing root causes, and promoting sustainable peace through education, development, reconciliation, and dialogue.*
- **Restorative justice:** *An approach to addressing conflicts and wrongdoing that focuses on repairing harm, promoting accountability, and restoring*

*relationships, rather than punishment.*

- **Sustainable development:** *The concept of meeting the needs of the present generation without compromising the ability of future generations to meet their own needs, integrating social, economic, and environmental dimensions.*
- **Dialogue:** *A process of communication and exchange of ideas between individuals or groups with different perspectives, aiming to promote understanding, bridge divides, and build common ground.*
- **Peace curriculum:** *The inclusion of peace education concepts, values, and skills in educational programs, encompassing formal and informal settings, to foster a culture of peace among learners.*
- **National identity:** *The sense of belonging and shared values that unite individuals within a nation, fostering a cohesive national identity.*
- **Patriotism:** *Love, loyalty, and devotion towards one's country, often involving a sense of pride in national symbols, history, and achievements.*
- **Civic education:** *The process of imparting knowledge, skills, and values related to citizenship, democracy, and national institutions, promoting active participation and responsible citizenship.*
- **Social cohesion:** *The degree of social unity and solidarity within a society, characterized by trust, cooperation, and mutual respect among diverse groups.*
- **Cultural diversity:** *The range of different cultures, traditions, languages, and customs within a society, emphasizing the importance of respecting and valuing diverse cultural identities.*
- **National language:** *The official or dominant language used in a country, often seen as a unifying factor for communication and expression of national identity.*
- **Constitutionalism:** *The adherence to constitutional principles, including the rule of law, separation of powers, and protection of individual rights, as a foundation for governance and national integration.*
- **Decentralization:** *The transfer of political, administrative, or economic power from central government to local or regional authorities, promoting participation and inclusivity.*
- **Inclusive policies:** *Policies that aim to address disparities, discrimination, and marginalization among different social, ethnic, or religious groups, promoting equal opportunities and social justice.*
- **National symbols:** *Icons, emblems, or symbols that represent the identity, unity, and values of a nation, such as the flag, national anthem, or national holidays.*
- **Globalization:** *The process of increased interconnectedness and*

*interdependence among countries, involving the exchange of goods, services, information, and ideas on a global scale.*

- **Regional integration:** *The process of countries within a specific geographic region coming together to foster closer economic, political, and social cooperation, such as the European Union or the Association of Southeast Asian Nations (ASEAN).*
- **Free trade:** *The removal or reduction of barriers (such as tariffs or quotas) to promote the flow of goods and services between countries, facilitating economic integration.*
- **Diplomacy:** *The practice of conducting negotiations, dialogue, and communication between countries to manage conflicts, build partnerships, and promote mutual understanding.*
- **Multilateralism:** *The principle of coordinating and cooperating with multiple countries or international organizations to address global challenges and promote shared interests.*
- **International law:** *The body of rules and principles that govern the conduct and relations between states, aiming to maintain peace, resolve conflicts, and promote human rights.*
- **Transnational organizations:** *Non-governmental organizations (NGOs), multinational corporations (MNCs), and international organizations (such as the United Nations) that operate across national borders, playing a role in global governance and integration.*
- **Migration:** *The movement of people from one country to another for various reasons, such as work, education, or seeking refuge, contributing to cultural exchange and demographic shifts.*
- **Global governance:** *The collective efforts and mechanisms for managing global affairs, addressing global challenges, and promoting cooperation among countries.*
- **Peace diplomacy:** *Diplomatic efforts aimed at preventing conflicts, resolving disputes, and fostering peaceful resolutions between nations, often involving negotiation, mediation, and peacebuilding initiatives.*
- **Accomodation:** *Adjustments made to teaching strategies, classroom environment or assessments to enable students with disabilities to participate fully and demonstrate their learning.*
- **Empathy:** *The ability to understand and share the feelings of others.*
- **Labor Force:** *The total number of people who are either employed or actively seeking employment.*
- **Generational Poverty:** *A cycle of poverty passed down through generations,*

*often linked to long term unemployment.*

- **Open Admission:** *A policy that allows students to enroll in courses or degree programs without strict entry requirements.*
- **E-learning:** *A broad term encompassing all forms of learning delivered economically.*
- **Massive Open Online Courses (MOOCs):** *Free, online courses offered by universities or other educational institutions that are open to a large number of participants globally.*

# REFERENCES & WEB REFERENCES

- Aggrawal, J.c. (2005). Education for Values, Environment and Human Rights.
- Dayakara Reddy & Digumarti Bhaskara Rao (2006). Value Oriented Education. New Delhi: Discovery Publishing House.
- Galtung, Johan (1975) Essays in Peace Research, Volume 1. Copenhagen: Eljers. pp. 334-339
- Manoj, K. (2008) Teaching of Human rights.
- Venkataiah, (2009). Value education. New Delhi: APH Publishing Corporation.
- Vessels, G., & Huitt, W. (2005). Moral and character development. Presented at the National Youth at Risk Conference, Savannah, GA, October 21, 2015. Retrieved from http://www.edpsycinteractive.org/brilstar/chapters/chardev.doc
- Yogesh Kumar Singh (2007). Value Education. New Delhi: APH Publishing Corporation.
- Rani, Ila. "Role of Education in Inculcation of Education For Peace." Issues and Ideas in Education 3, no. 2 (September 2, 2015): 103–16.
- http://dx.doi.org/10.15415/iie.2015.32008.
- http://shodhganga.inflibnet.ac.in/bitstream/10603/5067/11/11_chapter%201.pdf
- http://www.edpsycinteractive.org/topics/morchr/morchr.html
- http://iosrjournals.org/iosr-jhss/papers/ICAET-2014/volume-1/4.pdf
- https://www.researchgate.net/publication/259322707_Role_of_Parents_Guardians_and_Teachers_in_Value_Education
- http://shodhganga.inflibnet.ac.in/bitstream/10603/33620/7/07_chapter1.pdf
- http://ctb.ku.edu/en/table-of-contents/overview/model-for-community-change-andimprovement/core-principles-and-values/main
- http://unesdoc.unesco.org/images/0015/001580/158071eb.pdf

* 9 7 9 8 8 9 6 1 0 4 5 1 3 *